Small-Group Times to Scaffold Early Learning

Small-Group Times to Scaffold Early Learning

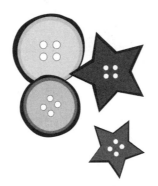

HighScope Early Childhood Staff
Ann S. Epstein, PhD
Suzanne Gainsley
Shannon D. Lockhart
Beth Marshall
Polly Neill
Karen (Kay) Rush

HIGHSCOPE
PRESS ®

Ypsilanti, Michigan

Published by

HighScope® Press
A division of the
HighScope Educational Research Foundation
600 North River Street
Ypsilanti, Michigan 48198-2898
Ph: 800.40.PRESS
Fax: 800.442.4FAX
press@highscope.org
highscope.org

Editor: Joanne Tangorra
Design and Production: Judy Seling of Seling Design
Photography:
Jan Dowling & Terri Mitchell — 134
Bob Foran — 1, 4, 51, 54, 57, 63, 68, 85, Back Cover
Gregory Fox — 2, 10, 19, 23, 25, 36, 97, 105, 114, 142
HighScope Staff — all other photos

ISBN 978-1-57379-410-7

Library of Congress Cataloging-in-Publication Data

Small-group times to scaffold early learning / HighScope early childhood staff, Ann S. Epstein ... [et al.].
    p. cm.
  Includes index.
  ISBN 978-1-57379-410-7 (soft cover : alk. paper) 1. Education, Preschool--Activity programs. 2. Group work in education. I. Epstein, Ann S. II. High/Scope Educational Research Foundation.
  LB1140.35.C74S53 2009
  372.139'5--dc22
                          2008051129

Printed in the United States of America

10 9 8 7 6 5 4

Contents

IV. Science and Technology 75

Activities

V. The Arts: Visual & Music 105

Activities: Visual Art

Activities: Music

About the Authors 152

Acknowledgments

A jointly written book such as *Small-Group Times to Scaffold Early Learning* involves collaboration at many levels. The authors would first like to thank one another for sharing the work, encouraging creativity, reigning in excess, and offering practical suggestions to make the activities useful to teachers in the classroom. We credit publications director Nancy Brickman with envisioning and proposing the project, and greatly appreciate the diligent efforts of our editor, Joanne Tangorra, for asking the questions that helped us sharpen and clarify our ideas. Special thanks go to the designer, Judy Seling, for turning our manuscript into an attractive and user-friendly product. Finally, we want to acknowledge the teachers and children who for many years have generously shared their experiences with our early childhood staff. The lessons they learned and imparted have helped us better understand the ideas, materials, and above all, the adult-child interactions, that make small-group times fun and effectively scaffold early learning.

Introduction: What Is Small-Group Time?

Most early childhood programs have a time each day when children gather together in a small group for a shared activity. The level of adult support during this time can vary widely, ranging from situations in which teachers control and direct the small-group time activity (e.g., conducting an academic-style lesson, instructing children on making a look-alike art project) to those where children are simply given some materials to explore and use without any adult guidance.

HighScope takes a balanced approach to small-group times. That is, small-group times are based on adult-initiated activities in which children are encouraged to explore materials and ideas in their own way, with adults sharing the excitement of their discoveries and scaffolding children's learning. This book presents 52 small-group activities, designed for HighScope and other developmentally based programs, that will engage young children and inspire teachers to explore the world of learning in a variety of content areas. You will find many ideas for the kinds of materials you can use for activities and the ways you can interact with children in educationally meaningful and appropriate ways.

What Does an Active Learning Small-Group Time Look Like?

Small-group time is a 10- to 15-minute segment of the HighScope daily routine in which classroom teachers meet with a consistent group of 8 to 10 children to participate in a teacher-initiated, hands-on learning experience. Small groups gather at a consistent, designated place each day. As a result, children know where to go on their own when this part of the daily routine begins. (If the activity will occur at a different location on a given day, the group meets first at the usual place and then moves to the alternate spot together.) Small-group gathering places might be a table (such as that used for planning, recall, or snacktime), the floor in one area of the room, or the couch and chairs in the reading area. In friendly climates, it might even be outdoors, under a tree!

At small-group time, adults introduce children to new materials, ideas, and activities.

In an active learning setting, adults provide the materials for children to explore, but children decide how to use them.

At small-group time, adults introduce children to new materials, ideas, and activities. Both children and adults actively engage with the materials and ideas in a variety of ways. Small-group time gives teachers an opportunity to observe and interact daily with the same group of children and provides children with regular peer contact and interactions. This consistency strengthens relationships and creates a supportive educational environment that supports and extends the learning experiences children have during the other parts of the day.

How Do Children Learn at Small-Group Time?

Small-group time activities are consistent with the rest of the HighScope Curriculum, which is founded on the principles and practices of "active participatory learning." In this approach, children engage in activities that build on their natural curi-osity and interests. They make choices about what and how to play with materials, use language to communicate their ideas, solve problems encountered in play, and are encouraged by adults who participate alongside them and listen, comment, and extend (scaffold) the children's language and ideas.

As they work with the materials during small-group activities, children make choices about how to use them. They talk with one another and the adult about what they are doing and seeing. The adult observes and comments on the children's actions and thoughts, refers children to one another for ideas and help, acknowledges and encourages each child's efforts, promotes independent problem-solving and, when necessary, assists children in carrying out their intentions. Children often work with the materials or extend their ideas from small-group time into work time (choice time) or other parts of the daily routine.

How Do Teachers Support Children at Small-Group Time?

To guarantee that children of all developmental levels have a positive learning experience during small-group time, HighScope teachers use the following *five ingredients essential for active learning:*

Materials. Programs offer abundant supplies of diverse, age-appropriate materials that are appealing to all the senses and are open ended, that is, they lend themselves to being used in a variety of ways and help expand children's experiences and stimulate their thinking. At small-group time, attention to this active-learning component means children encounter many types of materials, including some they might not choose to play with on their own and/or others that are being (re)introduced to the classroom. Depending on the activity, children are each given their own set of materials to work with and/or they are provided with easy access to shared materials.

Manipulation. Children handle, examine, combine, and transform materials and ideas. They make discoveries through direct hands-on and "minds-on" contact with these resources. At small-group time, the emphasis on manipulation means children experience materials directly, that is, they examine the physical properties of objects, handle things, listen to and make sounds, move their bodies, feel different textures, smell different aromas, taste different foods, and interact one-on-one and in a group context with peers and adults.

Choice. In an active learning setting, children have opportunities to make choices throughout the day. They choose materials and play partners, create and develop play ideas, and plan activities according to their current needs and expanding interests. The value of child choice during small-group time means children are free to explore materials and ideas in ways that are meaningful to them. They are not expected to use materials in a prescribed way or produce specific results that are determined by an adult. Teachers provide the materials, but children choose how to use them.

Child language and thought. Children describe what they are doing and what they understand about their experiences. They communicate verbally and nonverbally as they think about their behavior and modify their conclusions to take new learning into account. During small-group time, children talk about their actions and observations as they interact with materials and one another. They share their ideas and thoughts about their explorations and the effects they observe.

Adult scaffolding. Adults support children's current level of understanding, while challenging them to advance to the next stage of thinking and reasoning. In this way, adults help children gain knowledge, develop creative problem-solving skills, and reflect on what they are learning. As small-group time unfolds, teachers circulate among the children, supporting and extending their individual explorations and discoveries. They observe and imitate children's actions, repeat the words they use and extend their vocabularies, and pose open-ended questions that encourage children to try new things and consider the "what, how, and why" of their experiences. Adults also refer children to one another to share ideas and solve problems collaboratively.

In sum, when applied to small-group time, the five ingredients of active learning translate into adult support for children exploring materials, experimenting, building, creating and solving problems in their own ways. Young children talk about what they are doing and seeing, make discoveries, and share ideas with others. As a result, small-group experiences spark many ideas that extend to children's thinking and behavior throughout the program day and often to their lives outside of school. Small-group time thus serves as a springboard for development.

What Happens Before, During, and After Small-Group Time?

Adult planning. As part of daily team planning, teachers decide what they will do with the children during small-group time. (If there is more than one group in the classroom, each often does a different activity.) Teachers may get ideas for small-group time from many sources, including:

- Curriculum content
- Children's interests
- New, unexplored, underused, or favorite materials

To scaffold learning, adults support children's current level of thinking while challenging them to advance to the next stage.

- Local traditions and community events
- Teacher idea books and other curriculum materials

The ideas in this book are derived from and organized according to the HighScope Curriculum content, which is described in the manuals *Educating Young Children* (Hohmann, Weikart, & Epstein, 2008) and *Essentials of Active Learning in Preschool* (Epstein, 2007). Additional ideas for small-group times can be found in Graves (2007) and Marshall (2007), while resources specifically related to each curriculum content area covered in this book are included in the introductions to those chapters, respectively. You will also find many opportunities to incorporate other sources of ideas (including those listed above) and to carry out follow-up activities as you implement and think about the small-group activity plans presented here.

Preparing ahead of time. Once they have a plan clearly in mind — based, for example, on an activity in this book — teachers get ready for small groups ahead of time, often in the morning before children arrive. With advance teacher preparation, children do not have to wait to get started and can make good and interesting use of every minute of the session. Getting ready means two things. First is gathering the necessary materials, usually a set for each child and teacher; often teachers also make available shared and/or backup materials, and these are also prepared before children arrive. Second, since groups generally meet in an area used for other activities too, the materials are stored in a place where the adult can get to them easily and quickly as soon as small-group time begins (see sidebar, p. 5).

Carrying out the activity. When planning and preparing for small-group times, teachers

Gathering and Storing Small-Group-Time Materials

To facilitate collecting, storing, and distributing materials efficiently at small-group time, you can use the following containers to gather and sort supplies before the activity begins:

- Small plastic baskets
- Paper lunch sacks
- Large yogurt containers
- Margarine tubs
- Berry baskets
- Frozen-dinner trays
- Tops and bottoms of cardboard gift boxes
- Waxed or plastic milk cartons with tops cut off
- Egg cartons (good for sorting small items)
- Thin plastic flowerpots from bedding plants

Start your own collection of reusable containers and invite families to donate clean, recyclable items to the classroom.

---

think about the *beginning* of the session, that is, how they will introduce and distribute the materials. They think about the *middle,* or how they will support and extend children's learning. And they think about the *end,* that is, how they will bring the activity to a close, clean up materials, and make the transition to the next part of the day's routine. (For a summary of small-group time, see sidebar, p. 6.)

- **Beginning.** Children arrive eager to begin work, so teachers engage them as soon as they arrive at the gathering place. Teachers make a brief introductory statement or offer a simple challenge, such as *Today we have boxes in different sizes and some small, medium, and large bears. I wonder what we can do with them;* or *Let's see what we can find out about this book by looking at the picture on the cover.*
- **Middle.** Once children have begun to work with the materials, the teacher's role is to pay attention to their actions and ideas, scaffold learning, and encourage them to interact with and learn from one another. Adults do this by closely attending to each child, getting down to their physical level, watching and listening to them, imitating and building on their actions, and following their leads. They converse with children, asking questions sparingly, encouraging children to solve problems, and referring them to one another for ideas and assistance. Teachers also support children's highly individual use of materials and their observations about what they are doing and learning. In fact, one indication of an effective small-group time is the sheer variety of ideas the children come up with, often surprising their teachers!

In each of the small-group activities presented in this book, you will find examples of what children at different developmental levels — earlier, middle, and later — may say and do, and suggestions for how adults can support children at each of these levels. These examples and ideas are illustrative, not exhaustive, so as you carry out the activities, be alert to children's other behaviors and use the strategies presented here to spark and build on ideas of your own.

- **End.** Letting children know when small-group time is about to end (a two- or three-minute warning) gives them control over how to bring the session to closure. Some may be ready to stop while others may want to store what they are doing to continue at work time the following day. Also, while small group has a predetermined ending, children will nevertheless finish what they are doing at different times. On any given day, some children will be done with the materials and activity quickly, while others will want to linger. Teachers therefore schedule the day so children can move (transition) to the next segment as they are ready.

Following up. Children — and teachers — emerge from small groups with many ideas about how to continue and extend the excitement and learning that occurred during an activity. Based on what teachers see and hear from children, they may add new materials to the classroom, plan related small- or large-group activities, use part

Small-Group Time: A Summary

Sources of ideas for small-group time

1. Curriculum content
2. Children's interests
3. New, unexplored, underused, or favorite materials
4. Local traditions and community events
5. Teacher idea books and other curriculum materials

Preparation

1. Collect and organize the necessary materials and equipment ahead of time.
2. Store the materials in an easily accessible place.

Small-group time: Beginning

1. Have materials and equipment at the gathering place or bring them there.
2. Briefly introduce the materials, equipment, or activity by

   - Handing out the materials or calling attention to the equipment
   - Using the materials or equipment to play a game with the children
   - Telling a story using the materials or equipment
   - Posing a problem: Let's see what would happen if …

3. Let children begin working immediately.

Small-group time: Middle

1. Observe how children use or examine materials and equipment, and listen to what they say.
2. Use and examine materials and equipment yourself, imitating children.
3. Move from child to child and engage in conversations. If gathered around one item (such as a book or the computer), attend closely to each child and support his or her contribution to the conversation.
4. Refer children to one another for problem-solving.
5. Use a variety of adult-child interaction strategies to scaffold (support and extend) children's learning.

Small-group time: End

1. Give children a two- or three-minute warning.
2. Make cleaning up and putting away materials part of the activity.
3. Have children transition *actively* to the next activity.

Follow-up

1. Add new materials the classroom.
2. Plan related small- or large-group activities.
3. Use the activity as the basis for a planning or recall strategy.
4. Use the activity as the basis for a transition.
5. Support children's extensions of the activity at work/choice time or during other parts of the day.
6. Talk to parents about providing comparable materials and experiences at home.

of the activity as a basis for a planning or recall strategy, or take an idea and use it as the spark for an engaging transition. Perhaps the best indication that a small-group time has been successful is when children continue to use the materials and explore the ideas in their own ways during work/ choice time or other parts of the daily routine.

Parents can often provide comparable materials and experiences with their children at home as well. [For more information on extending children's learning at home, see Graves (2000) and the HighScope online series *All About HighScope* and *You and Your Child*.]

How This Book Is Organized

This book presents 52 small-group activities based on the HighScope *curriculum content* in five areas:

- Language, literacy, and communication
- Physical development, health, and well-being
- Mathematics
- Science and technology
- The Arts: Visual art and music

Each content area begins with a brief description of how children explore, master concepts, and develop skills in that domain of learning. This summary is followed by a set of complete activity descriptions to help teachers plan, carry out, and follow up each of the activities within that area.

Each small-group activity description follows a standard format and includes the following:

- **Title of activity** — the name of the activity
- **Content area** — the relevant content area that is the focus of the activity
- **Materials** — what teachers need to gather or prepare for each child as well as any shared or back-up materials
- **Beginning** — how to briefly introduce the activity to the children, expecting that they will use the materials and explore the ideas in their own ways
- **Middle** — how to acknowledge, support, and extend children's ideas at different developmental levels (earlier, middle, and later) with examples of what children may say and do at each level (from simply exploring materials to using and talking about them in complex ways) and the strategies adults can use to support their learning
- **End** — how to bring the activity to a close, let children know how they can continue to work with the materials and ideas, and transition to the next part of the daily routine
- **Ideas for follow-up** — ways to extend the learning experience throughout the indoor and outdoor classroom environment and the program day
- **Adaptations for children with special needs** — how to adapt the materials and/or activity so children with special needs can fully participate in the group-learning process

As you explore the activities contained in this book and other HighScope resources (see references at the end of this chapter and in the introductions to each content area), you will find many ideas for planning and carrying out small-group times that engage young children in active participatory learning in all the content areas of the curriculum. When you plan and share appropriate small-group experiences with the young children in your program, you will also discover that you have much to learn from them!

References

All About HighScope Fact Sheets. [Online]. *www.highscope.org*

Epstein, A. S. (2007). *Essentials of active learning in preschool: Getting to know the High/Scope Curriculum.* Ypsilanti, MI: HighScope Press.

Graves, M. (2000). *The teacher's idea book: The essential parent workshop resource.* Ypsilanti, MI: HighScope Press.

Graves, M. (2007). *Explore and learn quick cards: 80 activities for small groups.* Ypsilanti, MI: HighScope Press.

Hohmann, M., Weikart, D. P., & Epstein, A.S. (2008). *Educating young children: Active learning practices for preschool and child care programs.* (3rd ed.). Ypsilanti, MI: HighScope Press.

Marshall, B. (2007). *High/Scope step by step: Lesson plans for the first 30 days.* Ypsilanti, MI: HighScope Press.

You and Your Child (Parent Newsletter Series). [Online]. *www.highscope.org*

I. Language, Literacy, and Communication

Early literacy is an important foundation of school readiness because so much later learning depends on the ability to read. Knowing how to read is, in turn, highly dependent on language skills, particularly vocabulary. Understanding and using oral language (listening and speaking) is the first step in mastering printed language (reading and writing). Communication in all its forms — spoken, written, and gestural — is a way to transmit information as well as the basis of relationships. Young children communicate to make their needs known, form social bonds, express feelings, share their observations and thoughts, and learn from others about the world around them. Language and communication are therefore intertwined with all areas of individual development, and they are essential to children becoming members of their family, classroom, and other social groups.

The development of language and literacy begins at birth. Newborns and young infants produce an amazing array of sounds. Older infants and toddlers say words to communicate their needs and relate to caregivers and peers. During preschool, language is increasingly used to establish and maintain relationships. Three- and four-year-olds converse, ask questions, consider what they hear, describe and reflect on their surroundings, refer to things that are not present, talk about desires, and construct imaginary situations. Their vocabularies are growing and they are mastering the basic rules of grammar. Young children are also beginning to read and write. They do this in unconventional ways at first (such as "reading" pictures and scrib-

Children acquire language and literacy skills because they want to communicate with others.

bling horizontal lines they call "writing"), but they are also eager to learn the conventions of reading and writing used in their society.

Emerging Literacy in Young Children

In the past three decades, researchers such as Catherine Snow, Susan Burns, and Peg Griffin (1998) have written a great deal about how language and literacy develop in young children. Reading instruction used to begin in first grade. However, as studies showed the connection between spoken and written language, we came to understand that literacy "emerges" gradually in the early years, beginning in infancy with learning to talk and looking at books. Preschool continues (and, in some cases, fills the gaps in) this process. A good early literacy curriculum prepares preschool children for more formal reading instruction in their elementary years.

In its landmark review of the research, the National Reading Panel (2000) identified four components of early literacy development that are especially critical in the early years:

- **Phonological awareness.** The ability to attend to the sounds of language as distinct from its meaning, phonological awareness encompasses *phonemic awareness,* which develops when children are able to hear and break words into phonemes (a phoneme is the smallest unit of sound, such as the /b/ in *ball*). Phonemic awareness in children is characterized by the ability to detect *rhymes* (the same pattern at the end of two or more words) and *alliteration* (the repetition of the initial sound in groups of words).
- **Comprehension.** This is the process of making meaning of spoken and written language by connecting what one is learning to what one already knows.
- **Concepts about print.** Also called *print awareness,* this early literacy component refers to how print is organized and used in reading and writing, for example, how print appears on the page and in the parts of a book.
- **Alphabetic principle.** Children apply this principle when they understand that there is

Before they begin to reproduce the letters of the alphabet, children often make up their own symbols and letterlike forms.

a systematic relationship between letters and sounds, recognize letter names and their accompanying sounds, and understand that whole words are made up of groups of individual sounds.

HighScope teacher-educator Linda Weikel Ranweiler, in her book *Preschool Readers and Writers: Early Literacy Strategies for Teachers* (2004), further underscores the lessons that early childhood educators need to keep in mind as they help children hone the above emergent literacy skills:

- Language and literacy are connected from infancy onward. Speaking, listening, reading, and writing develop concurrently (together) rather than sequentially (one after the other).
- The acquisition of language and literacy skills is social. It happens because young children want to interact and communicate with others.
- Literacy learning occurs during meaningful interactions, experiences, and activities.
- Children differ in how — and how fast — they learn. For example, some children readily pick up the sounds of language, while others need

more time and more formal instruction to develop this phonological awareness.

- Much language and literacy learning happens naturally during play and everyday experiences, while some depends on explicit (intentional) instruction from observant and sensitive adults.

- Differences in home language and culture can affect literacy development. An effective program of support and instruction allows for these differences, for example, helping children make the connection between the vocabulary of their home language(s) and the words used at school.

The HighScope Curriculum takes all these findings into account, and the small-group activities on the following pages emphasize the strong association between language and literacy development. For more ideas about how to support this important area of development, see the *Growing Readers Early Literacy Curriculum* (HighScope Educational Research Foundation, 2005; 2007), a set of small-group activities and other daily learning experiences designed for all developmentally based preschool programs (not only those using HighScope). Related publications include *Fee, Fie, Phonemic Awareness* (Hohmann, 2002), *Letter Links* (DeBruin-Parecki & Hohmann, 2003), *Letter Links Online* (HighScope, 2009), *Storybook Talk* (Hohmann & Adams, 2008), and *From Message to Meaning: Using a Daily Message Board in the Preschool Classroom* (Gainsley, 2008). To assess children's progress in developing language and literacy skills, see the *Early Literacy Skills Assessment* (ELSA; HighScope Educational Research Foundation, 2004).

References

DeBruin-Parecki, A., & Hohmann, M. (2003). *Letter Links: Alphabet learning with children's names*. Ypsilanti, MI: HighScope Press.

Gainsley, S. (2008). *From message to meaning: Using a daily message board in the preschool classroom*. (Book and DVD). Ypsilanti, MI: HighScope Press.

HighScope Educational Research Foundation. (2004). *Early Literacy Skills Assessment*. Ypsilanti, MI: HighScope Press.

HighScope Educational Research Foundation. (2005). *Growing Readers Early Literacy Curriculum*. Ypsilanti, MI: HighScope Press.

HighScope Educational Research Foundation. (2007). *Growing Readers Early Literacy Curriculum: Set 2*. Ypsilanti, MI: HighScope Press.

HighScope Educational Research Foundation. *Letter Links Online*. (2009). [Online]. Ypsilanti, MI: HighScope Press.

Hohmann, M. (2002). *Fee, fie, phonemic awareness: 130 prereading activities for preschoolers*. Ypsilanti, MI: HighScope Press.

Hohmann, M., & Adams, K. (2008). *Storybook talk: Conversations for comprehension*. Ypsilanti, MI: HighScope Press.

National Reading Panel. (2000). *Teaching children to read: An evidence-based assessment of the scientific research literature on reading and its implications for reading instruction*. Washington, DC: National Institute of Child Health and Human Development, National Institutes of Health.

Ranweiler, L. (2004). *Preschool readers and writers: Early literacy strategies for teachers*. Ypsilanti, MI: HighScope Press.

Snow, C. E., Burns, S., and Griffin, P. (Eds.). (1998). *Preventing reading difficulties in young children*. Washington, DC: National Academy Press.

▌ Drawing the Story

Children listen to a familiar story, talk about characters and events in the story and what they think might happen next (after the story ends), and draw a picture about the story.

Time of day: Small-Group Time | **Content Area:** Language, Literacy, and Communication

Materials

Materials for each child and teacher:

- 1 sheet of drawing paper
- Assorted drawing implements such as crayons, markers, chalk, or oil pastels

Shared materials:

- Familiar storybook (book with characters and plot)

Backup materials:

- If possible, extra copies of the same story

Beginning

- Read or retell a familiar story with children, drawing attention to the pictures in the book.
- Ask children to remember what happens next during the story, that is, what they remember from having heard the story before.
- At the end of the story, ask children what they think might happen next to the main character (e.g., *Will* [name of main character] *take another adventure? What will* [name of main character] *do next?*).
- Acknowledge the children's responses.

Middle

- Give children a sheet of paper and drawing implement.
- Ask children to draw a picture about the story or a picture about what might happen next if the story were to continue.

End

- Ask children to move like a character from the story to the next part of the daily routine.

Ideas for follow-up

- Revisit the story with individual children or small groups at greeting time. Encourage children to picture-read the story (retelling the story by looking at the pictures).
- Repeat the activity with other book(s) and use three-dimensional art materials (e.g., play dough, modeling clay).

Adaptations for children with special needs

- Use books with large pictures.
- Use adaptive devices (like a writing splint) so children can successfully hold a crayon or marker.

During this activity, children listen to a familiar storybook and then draw pictures related to the story.

Developmental range: Supporting children at different levels

Earlier ————————→   **Middle** ————————→   **Later** ————————→

Children may

- Draw a picture and talk about an unrelated topic.
- Name characters in the story.
- Tell one or two details that happened in the story (e.g., *The baby bear cried*).
- Make a brief comment that connects the story to real life (e.g., *I saw bears in the zoo*).

Adults can

- Name the characters in the story (e.g., *I remember there was a girl named* Goldilocks *and a papa bear*).
- Say, *Help me remember what happened in the story.*
- Mention a part of the story that they enjoyed (e.g., *It was interesting that Goldilocks always tried what belonged to all three bears — the papa, the mama, and the baby*).

Children may

- Draw a picture representation of the story (does not have to be recognizable).
- Tell three or more details of the story.
- Connect objects or events from the story to their own experience (e.g., *I don't like porridge. I like pancakes*).
- Give an idea about what might happen if the story were to continue (e.g., *The bears will chase Goldilocks*).

Adults can

- Say, *Tell me about your picture.*
- Ask, *What part did you like in the story?*
- Say, *I wonder what* [name of character] *does after* [last event] (e.g., *I wonder what Goldilocks does after she runs away from the bears' house*).

Children may

- Tell two or three ideas to continue the story (e.g., *The bears chase Goldilocks because they are mad at her. Then Goldilocks goes in her house and locks the door*).
- Relate events/characters in the story to themselves (e.g., *If the bears chased me, I would jump on my dirt bike and ride away fast*).
- Contribute to conversations of others in the group.

Adults can

- Ask, *Why does* [name of character] *do that?*
- Ask children what they would do if they were in the predicament of the story.
- Write down a child's new story on a separate sheet of paper and attach it to the child's drawing.
- Refer children to one another (e.g., *Sammy also drew a picture of what Goldilocks did after she ran away from the bears' house. Let's look at both of your pictures*).

2 Field Trip Story

Adults take dictation from children as they together create a story about a recent field trip; children make drawings to illustrate the story. [Note: This activity should be done the day after a field trip, or as soon as possible following the trip, when the experience is still fresh in the children's minds.]

Time of day: Small-Group Time   **Content Area:** Language, Literacy, and Communication

Materials

Materials for each child and teacher:
- Drawing paper
- Markers

Shared materials:
- Large pieces of paper (e.g., chart paper) folded in half to make a large book
- Markers

Backup materials:
- Photos (or other artifacts) from the field trip

Beginning
- Tell the children that you would like them to help you create a story about their recent trip to the _____.
- Encourage children to think of a title for the story.
- Begin the story with an opening sentence such as *One day our class went to the _____,* or *Once upon a time we took a trip to the _____.*

Middle
- Help children recall events of the trip, and write down their words in the chart paper book.
- Read back the words you have written.
- Give children drawing paper and markers to draw illustrations for the story.

End
- Read the story to the children from the beginning. As you read, follow the line of print with your finger.
- Add children's drawings to the book. Ask children to tell you where in the story to insert the drawings so that they correspond to the text.

- Ask children to move like something they saw on the field trip to the next part of the daily routine.

Ideas for follow-up
- Hang up the story in the classroom or make a class field trip book by typing the story and placing it in a binder with the children's pictures.
- At recall time, create a group story about what children did at work time.
- Encourage parents to create books with their children about routines, outings, and events that are meaningful to the family.

Adaptations for children with special needs
- Make sure children with vision or hearing limitations are close enough to see and hear the story being created.
- Encourage children with communicative difficulties to gesture or act out meaningful parts of their trip, while you or other children describe these ideas in words. Also encourage nonverbal children to draw events and/or experiences they recall from the field trip.

Developmental range: Supporting children at different levels

Earlier ⟶   **Middle** ⟶   **Later** ⟶

Children may

- Listen to other children's comments.
- Name something seen or done on the field trip using a single word or short phrase.
- Repeat what other children say.
- Draw with markers.

Adults can

- Acknowledge children's contributions by repeating their words (e.g., *Jacob remembers the tractor*).
- Write down children's words and comment on their response to what children say (e.g., *You said* tractor, *and I wrote the word* tractor).
- Comment on children's drawings and relate them to the trip (e.g., *You're using the red crayon. We saw a red barn on the trip to the farm*).

Children may

- Talk about people seen and events that happened on the trip using descriptive language and sentences.
- Identify letters written on the paper.
- Make the initial letter sound of a word.
- Draw something related to the field trip.

Adults can

- Encourage children to elaborate on their descriptions (e.g., *Yes, those chickens were really noisy! What should we write about the sound they made?*).
- Point to each word while reading back sentences.
- Emphasize the initial sounds in some words that children say (e.g., Tractor *starts with the /t/ sound*).
- Ask *What letter makes that sound?*

Children may

- Make a comment and say, *Write that down!*
- Identify the beginning letter of a word (e.g., Tractor *starts with a* t. *Make the letter* t).
- Recognize/read a written word.
- Draw and write something related to field trip.

Adults can

- Ask children to give them suggestions for words to write down.
- Encourage children to help them spell words by identifying the beginning and ending sounds and letters of words.
- If asked, help children spell words (e.g., tell them the letters, write words for them to copy).
- Ask children to read back what they have written.

Following a field trip, children create a group story about the outing as adults take dictation. Children then draw pictures to illustrate the story.

3 Greeting Cards

Children make greeting cards for friends and family members, using (un)conventional forms of writing (lines and squiggles, letters and letterlike forms, invented and real spelling).

Time of day: Small-Group Time   **Content Area:** Language, Literacy, and Communication

Materials

Materials for each child and teacher:
- Greeting cards, stationery, unused invitations
- Writing implements
- Names and letter links or symbols of children in the class

Shared materials:
- None

Backup materials:
- Envelopes

Beginning
- Show children a selection of greeting cards and talk about sending and receiving cards. Ask children about occasions and circumstances when they have given or received cards (e.g., on birthdays and holidays, as invitations, to say "thank you" or "get well").
- Give children a selection of greeting cards and markers or other writing implements and suggest that they write a card to someone.

Middle
- Encourage children's developmental writing (i.e., from marks and squiggles to letters and words).
- Give children envelopes.

End
- Suggest that children who have made cards for classmates deliver their cards to their classmates' cubbies. If they've written cards for family members, suggest they put them in their cubbies to take home.

- Ask children to transition to the next activity based on the type of cards they've written or to whom they've written (e.g., *If you wrote a card to* [someone in the class, the teacher, to someone in your family, etc.], *go to the next activity.* Or *If you wrote* [a birthday card, a party invitation, a get-well card, etc.], *go to* [the next activity].

Ideas for follow-up
- Add greeting cards and envelopes to the writing area of your classroom.
- Make a mailbox for the classroom.
- At planning (or recall) time, label envelopes with each of the areas of the classroom. Ask children to place their name card in the envelope that corresponds to the area where they will play (or played) at work time.

Adaptations for children with special needs
- For children whose visual impairments prevent them from writing, encourage them to dictate their messages. Record them and play them back.
- Include large greeting cards and broad-gesture writing tools (e.g., brushes) to encourage and enable children with motor or coordination problems to write.

Developmental range: Supporting children at different levels

Earlier ⟶　　**Middle** ⟶　　**Later** ⟶

Children may

- Look at, open, and close cards.
- Talk about what they see on their cards.
- Draw on their cards using scribble writing.
- Say who their card is for.

Adults can

- Talk with children about what they see on the card (e.g., *I see balloons on this card. I think it might be a birthday card*).
- Notice children's writing (e.g., *I see you did some writing on your card*).
- Talk about the card they are writing and who it's for; write that person's name on the card, and write and read aloud the card's message to the children.

Children may

- Talk about occasions when they have received cards.
- Notice the words on the cards.
- Write letters or letterlike forms on their cards.
- Read their own writing.

Adults can

- Talk about occasions when they have received cards.
- Ask children about their writing (e.g., *Tell me what your card says*).
- Ask children to suggest words they might include on their card (e.g., *love, to, from, hello*).

Children may

- Write their name and/or someone else's name (e.g., teacher, friend, family member) on a card.
- Ask how to spell one or more words.
- Copy words.
- Sound out words and write corresponding letters (invented spelling).

Adults can

- Provide name cards for children to copy.
- Write down other words for children to copy.
- Encourage children to identify the beginning sounds of words.
- Give children envelopes and encourage them to write the name of the recipient on the envelope.

4 Jack Be Nimble, Jack Be Quick

Children listen to the nursery rhyme "Jack Be Nimble," then "jump" a small doll figure over a candlestick and other items as they create their own rhymes for Jack.

Time of day: Small-Group Time

Content Area: Language, Literacy, and Communication

Materials

Materials for each child and teacher:

- Candle in a holder
- Small doll figure to represent Jack
- Other items for Jack to jump over, such as books, blocks, carpet squares, and pillows

Shared materials:

- None

Backup materials:

- Tape measures

Beginning

- Use the small doll to tell the children a story about a boy named Jack who loved to jump, especially over candlesticks.
- Say the nursery rhyme "Jack Be Nimble" as you demonstrate how Jack jumps over the candlestick.

    Jack be nimble, Jack be quick
    Jack jump over the candlestick.

- Repeat the rhyme and encourage the children to say it with you.
- Give each of the children a doll figure and a candlestick to practice jumping over.

Middle

- Give the children other items to jump over using their doll and say *Let's see if we can make up some other rhymes for Jack.* For example:

    Jack be nimble, Jack be hook
    Jack jump over the book.

- Listen to and encourage the rhymes children make up. Accept made-up words as well as real words (e.g., *drock* and *clock*). Encourage children to substitute their own names for Jack and/or other actions besides jumping.

End

- After children have cleaned up their materials, make up a rhyme and encourage them to "jump" to their next activity, for example, *Class be nimble, class be able, everybody jump to the snack table* or *Class be nimble, class be wide, now let's get ready to go outside.* You can use the word *rhyme* to rhyme with *time.* If you cannot think of a real rhyming word, use a made-up word.

Ideas for follow-up

- Act out other nursery rhymes at small-group time or large-group time.
- Say or sing nursery rhymes with children throughout the day (e.g., when they are swinging on the swings, at the snack table, making transitions).
- Include books with nursery rhymes and other rhymes in the reading/book area. When you read these with children and they become familiar with them, encourage them to think of other rhyming words at the ends of the lines.

Adaptations for children with special needs

- Encourage nonmobile children to think of upper body movements for Jack or movements they can perform with their assistive devices (e.g., rhyme words with *wheel, slide,* or *roll*). Encourage them to use doll figures to act out other rhymes.

Developmental range: Supporting children at different levels

Earlier ————————————▶ **Middle** ————————————▶ **Later** ————————————▶

Earlier

Children may
- Jump or move their doll over objects.
- Say part of the rhyme.

Adults can
- Acknowledge children's actions (e.g., *Your doll is jumping just like Jack*).
- Say the rhyme as children make jumping movements with their doll; ask children if they would like to say the rhyme together.

Middle

Children may
- Recite the rhyme.
- Say that two words rhyme (e.g., Quick *and* stick, *that rhymes*).

Adults can
- Point out the rhyming words (e.g., *Listen to these words* quick *and* stick. *They rhyme. They have the* ick *sound at the end*).
- Encourage children to think of other words that rhyme with *quick* and *stick*, (e.g., *What other words have the* ick *sound at the end?*).

Later

Children may
- Say other words that rhyme with *quick*, including made-up words (e.g., Brick *also rhymes with* quick! *or How about* drick? *That's a rhyme*).
- Make up other rhyming pairs (e.g., ... *Jack be* clock, *Jack jump over the* block).

Adults can
- Ask children to pick out the rhyming words (e.g., *I hear a word that rhymes with* quick. *Can you hear it?*).
- Say, *You jumped over the book. Can you think of something that rhymes with* book — *with the* ook *sound at the end?*

Teachers can keep books that feature rhymes in the book area and encourage children to make up their own rhyming words when they get to the end of a line.

5 Letter Links

Children match letters to pictures of symbols that start with the same letter and sound.

Time of day: Small-Group Time   **Content Area:** Language, Literacy, and Communication

Materials

Materials for each child and teacher:

- Set of letter-linked symbols, copied from *Letter Links* (or *Letter Links Online*) or drawn on 3" x 5" index cards; each set should contain a pair of (2) letter-linked symbols for each child in the small group (for a group of 8 children, each card set would contain 8 pairs of letter links)
- Small felt boards, carpet squares, or placemats to use as work space

Shared materials:

- None

Backup materials:

- Blank index cards and markers

Beginning

- Select three pairs of letter-linked symbols and place each symbol face down on a placemat in front of you. Turn one symbol over and say something like *Look, it's* [child's name] *symbol. See, here is the letter* [ ] *and a picture of a* [ ] *which begins with the* [/ /] *sound. I wonder if I can find one that matches.*
- Turn over other letter-linked symbols until you have matched all three pairs.
- Give children a container with letter-linked symbols and say *Here are some cards with letters and matching pictures for you to use on your placemat.*

Middle

- After children have had the opportunity to explore their letter-linked cards, introduce blank cards and markers and suggest that they might like to make their own cards.

End

- Ask children to place their letter-linked cards back in their baskets.
- Transition to the next activity using the initial sounds of children's names (e.g., *If your name starts with the* /s/ *sound, go to* [the next activity]; *If your name starts with the* /m/ *sound, go to* [the next activity], and so on.

Ideas for follow-up

- Use letter-linked pictures on children's coat hooks and cubbies.
- Create index cards with children's names on one side and letter-linked symbols on the other side. Put cards on a binder ring and make it available in the classroom.
- Refer to letter sounds throughout the day (e.g., *If your name starts with* /m/, *like* motorcycle *and* mitten, *wash your hands for snack; If your name starts with* /b/, *it's your turn to plan* [or *recall*]).

Adaptations for children with special needs

- Laminate children's name cards for durability.
- Use large index cards and large print for children with visual impairments.
- Sign the letters and corresponding (linked) symbols. [Note: Signing is an effective language-learning tool for young children with typically developing as well as limited hearing.]

Developmental range: Supporting children at different levels

Earlier ————→

Children may
- Name or talk about the pictures on the letter-linked cards.
- Identify their own letter link.
- Identify a letter as *a letter*.
- Draw on a blank card.

Adults can
- Name letter-linked symbols and identify the children they belong to, emphasizing the sound of the initial letter in the name and the symbol.
- Point out the letter on the child's letter-linked symbol (e.g., *This is your lion symbol and that is the letter* L. L *is the first letter in* Leon. Leon *and* lion *both start with the letter* L *and the* /l/ *sound*).

Middle ————→

Children may
- Identify a letter-linked symbol as belonging to a particular child (e.g., *That's Madison's moon*).
- Identify letters.
- Make the sound of a letter.
- Use scribble writing on a blank card and explain what it represents.

Adults can
- Point to a letter-linked card and note the connection between the picture and the child's name (e.g., Madison *and* moon *both start with the* /m/ *sound*).
- Point to a letter and make its sound.
- Encourage children to draw their own name (especially the first letter) and/or letter-linked symbol on a blank card.

Later ————→

Children may
- Identify the first letter of a word (e.g., *Heart starts with an* H).
- Recognize that two objects have the same initial letter.
- List two or more words that start with the same letter or sound.
- Draw letters and/or symbols on blank cards.

Adults can
- Say a letter sound and ask the child to find the corresponding picture (e.g., *I see something that starts with the* /b/ *sound*).
- Ask children to think of other words that begin with a particular letter.
- Encourage children to make up new letter-linked symbols for specific letters (e.g., *What picture could we use that starts with* P *and makes the* /p/ *sound?*).

As a follow-up to this activity, teachers can label children's coat hooks and cubbies with letter-links — pictures that begin with the same letter and sound as the first letter of their name.

6 Looking at Photos

Children talk about photographs of themselves and classmates as the teacher asks questions and adds to children's words and vocabulary.

Time of day: Small-Group Time   **Content Area:** Language, Literacy, and Communication

Materials

Materials for each child and teacher:

- Copies of photographs of children taken during classroom activities or on a recent field trip (use copy machine to copy more than one picture per page or, if using digital pictures, format multiple pictures per page)

Shared materials:

- None

Backup materials:

- Scissors

Beginning

- Tell the children that you have taken photographs of them at school or on a recent field trip.
- Give children sheets of paper on which you have printed copies of photos.
- Comment on one or two of the photos (e.g., *Here's a picture of us getting on the bus; This photo was taken at large-group time yesterday. Let's see what everyone was doing*).

Middle

- Listen to and talk with children about the photographs.
- Repeat children's words and add to their vocabulary using names of objects, people, and actions; descriptive words (e.g., physical properties, categories); time-related and sequencing words (e.g., *first, next, last, before, after*); and feeling words.
- Give children scissors to cut out photos they would like to keep.

End

- Have children put away the photos they would like to keep.
- Collect remaining photographs to put in a class photo album.
- Hold up a photo and tell the children that if they are in the photograph, they can move to the next part of the day. Hold up other photos and repeat the same process until all children have made the transition to the next activity.

Ideas for follow-up

- Place photos in a class photo album, or insert them into page protectors and put them in a binder.
- Have children create captions to go with each photograph.

Adaptations for children with special needs

- Enlarge photos to aid children with visual impairments.
- Copy photos onto cardstock or glue photos onto tagboard to make them sturdier for handling.

Developmental range: Supporting children at different levels

Earlier ⟶

Children may
- Look at photos and identify self and others by pointing (e.g., pointing and saying *That's her*).
- Point to and name objects or people in the photos.
- Describe actions happening in the photo (e.g., *She's running*).

Adults can
- Name people or objects that children point to.
- Use descriptive words to talk about photos (e.g., *That's the shiny red fire engine*).
- Describe what is happening in the photo (e.g., *The firefighter is lifting Jacob onto the truck*).

Middle ⟶

Children may
- Use descriptive words to talk about photos (e.g., *The fire truck is yellow, not red!*).
- Make a connection between something in the photo and their own life experience (e.g., *I have a fire truck at home*).
- Ask a question about what's happening in the photo (e.g., *Why do they have three refrigerators?*).

Adults can
- Ask children, *What do you see in this photo?*
- Describe specific things in the photo and ask children to guess what they are (e.g., *I spy something on the fire truck that is silver and round*).
- Make connections between objects or events in the photo with real-life experiences (e.g., *I live close to a fire station. I hear the sirens all the time*).

Later ⟶

Children may
- Use specific vocabulary related to the subject of the photo (e.g., *The firefighters have oxygen tanks so they can breathe*).
- Retell a sequence of events related to the pictures (e.g., *The firefighter opened the hose and then water squirted out on Ben*).
- Make comments that include two or more ideas (e.g., *If there's a fire in my house, I have a smoke detector that goes* beep, beep, beep. *Then I run out the door*).
- Talk with others about the photos.

Adults can
- Introduce vocabulary related to particular topics (e.g., *I remember the firefighter called that the hook-and-ladder truck*).
- Encourage children to talk in detail about the photos; comment on and ask follow-up questions (e.g., *Help me remember what happened before this; What were you and Brian so busy talking about here?*).
- Ask children to help you put a few photos in order according to the sequence of events. Talk about the order using vocabulary words such as *first, next, last*.

Photos of children engaged in different classroom activities can be placed in a class album. Children can create captions for them.

7 Looking for Letters

In this activity, children find letters on newspaper pages and circle them with markers.

Time of day: Small-Group Time   **Content Area:** Language, Literacy, and Communication

Materials

Materials for each child and teacher:

- Newspaper pages with large-type headlines, captions, or advertisements (not small-print classified ads)
- 2–3 markers

Shared materials:

- None

Backup materials:

- Children's name cards
- Catalogs, magazines, or other printed materials with large-type letters
- Scissors, paper, and tape

Beginning

- Talk to children about different items that have letters on them (e.g., books, signs, clothing). Hold up a newspaper page and remark on all the letters and words on the page.
- Have children point to and/or name three or four of the letters. If they cannot name some or ask for help, name those letters for them. Circle each of the named letters with a marker.

Middle

- Give children newspaper pages and markers and suggest that they might want to find and circle letters on the pages.
- Offer scissors, paper, and tape to children who want to cut out and arrange or attach their letters on a page.

End

- Send children to the next activity based on the first letter sound (or letter) in their name (e.g., *If your name begins with the* /b/ *sound, go to* [the next activity]; *If your name begins with the letter* M, *go to* [the next activity]; on so on).

Ideas for follow-up

- Put unused print materials (e.g., newspapers, catalogs, magazines) in the art area.
- Plan a small-group activity using newspaper, scissors, tape, and glue for children to make letter collages.
- Point out letters in the environment (e.g., *Look! That sign has an* E *at the beginning of the word, just like Ellie's name. It says* Exit).
- Use letter names and sounds as part of transition games (e.g., *When you hear the word that starts with the* /m/ *sound, go to your planning table*).

Adaptations for children with special needs

- Give children with visual limitations or motor difficulties only one or two half-sized pieces of newspaper with large headlines.
- Tape paper to the table to keep it from moving while children look for and/or circle letters.

Developmental range: Supporting children at different levels

Earlier ⟶

Children may
- Draw on paper without mentioning letters.
- Point to or draw around letters and say *Look at my letters* or ask *What's this?*
- Use letter names but not always correctly.
- Recognize a letter but not say the letter name (e.g., *That's my letter.* [Ashley points to the letter A]).

Adults can
- Acknowledge children's drawing while naming the letters on the page(s) (e.g., *You are drawing over the letters on the paper. You drew over* A *and* B *and* C).
- Name letters for children (e.g., *That's the letter* A).
- Encourage children to find matching letters (e.g., *Here's another* A. *I wonder if we can find more*).

Middle ⟶

Children may
- Identify uppercase letters.
- Say that a familiar word, such as a name, begins with a particular letter and identify the letter (e.g., M *is for* Momma).
- Ask, *What does this say?* (i.e., understand that print carries meaning).

Adults can
- Give children name cards and encourage them to find the letters of their name.
- Say, *I spy the first letter in Joshua's name. Can you find it?*
- Read headlines and captions aloud, pointing to each word.

Later ⟶

Children may
- Identify some lowercase letters.
- Identify a letter based on its sound.
- Say several words that start with the same letter (e.g., B *is for* baby, Brianna, backpack. *They all start with* B).

Adults can
- Point to and identify lowercase letters.
- Make the sound of a letter and encourage children to find the letter on the page (e.g., *I spy the letter that makes the* /b/ *sound, as in the word* ball).
- Encourage children to think of words that begin with a specific letter.

Some children circle the letters they find in the newspaper, while others may use scissors to cut them out and arrange them on paper.

8 Making Books

Children create books using blank booklets and pictures from magazines.

Time of day: Small-Group Time

Content area: Language, Literacy, and Communication

Materials

Materials for each child and teacher:

- Blank paper stapled or folded into books
- Variety of pages from various magazines with pictures of interest to children (e.g., pets, playgrounds, toys, food, construction sites, people of all ages and backgrounds)
- Scissors
- Glue sticks

Shared materials:

- None

Backup materials:

- Crayons, markers, or pencils

Beginning

- Hold up one of the blank booklets you have made and pretend that you are going to read it to the children. Stop and say something like *Wait a minute, I can't read this book. It's missing some things!* Acknowledge children's ideas about what the book is missing (e.g., words, pictures, title).
- Tell the children that you have blank books for them and some pictures they might like to cut out for their books.

Middle

- Encourage children to look at and cut out magazine pictures for their books. Cut out pictures yourself and talk about what you are doing.
- Mention that some books also have words with the book's title and a story about the characters. Some something like *I want to write a title for my book on the cover. What should I call it?* Write down a title the children suggest and read it back, pointing to each word. Offer crayons to children if they want to write in their books.

End

- As children are finishing, suggest that they might want to put their books in the book area for others to read or take them home to read to their parents.
- Transition to the next activity by dismissing children according to the content of their book (e.g., *If you wrote some letters in your book, you can get ready to go outside. If you glued a picture of a car into your book, you can go outside*).

Ideas for follow-up

- Create a group planning or recall book. Write down what children say they plan to do or what they did during work time.
- Add wordless picture books to the classroom and encourage children to talk about the pictures or make up a story.
- Write down children's stories as they tell them. Stories might be related to real-life events, based on movies they've seen, or simply made up.
- Suggest that children might like to draw a picture about their story.

Adaptations for children with special needs

- Encourage children with visual impairments for whom writing is difficult to dictate letters, words, and sentences to you. Read the dictation back to them. Record their "talking book" ideas, and play the tape back to them. Talk with them about their ideas for a title for their book.

Developmental range: Supporting children at different levels

Earlier ⟶　　　**Middle** ⟶　　　**Later** ⟶

Earlier

Children may
- Look at magazine pictures and/or cut them out but not put them in their book.
- Identify objects in the magazine pictures.
- Glue magazine pictures at random into their book (e.g., put all of them on the same page, skip pages).
- Turn pages of their book, several pages at a time.

Adults can
- Acknowledge the pictures children find or cut out (e.g., *You like cutting. You are even cutting your booklet*).
- Cut out and describe a magazine picture (e.g., *I'm cutting out a girl on a tricycle*).
- Ask, *What did you glue on the page of your book?*
- Comment to child turning pages of a book, *You are turning one page at a time.*

Middle

Children may
- Glue pictures onto pages of their book in order (e.g., begin on the first page and put pictures on some or all subsequent pages).
- Use descriptive words to talk about pictures.
- Look at their book by turning pages one at a time from front to back.
- Use scribble writing or make letterlike forms on the pages of the book.

Adults can
- Say, *Tell me about the pictures in your book.*
- Use terms such as *first page, next page,* and *last page* to emphasize the order in which the pages of books are read.
- Ask, *Does your book need any words?*
- Ask children about their writing and what it says.
- Offer to write down children's ideas.

Later

Children may
- Pretend to tell a story by talking about pictures and turning the pages in their book.
- Write some letters and letterlike forms in a line on the page.
- Write some familiar words in their book.

Adults can
- Say, *Tell me about your story.*
- Encourage children to think of a title for their book.
- Support children's sound spelling of words by helping them identify initial letter sounds.

Children cut photos from magazines, catalogs, and other printed materials to include in the books they make.

9 Retelling "The Three Little Pigs"

Children participate in a retelling of a popular folk tale, building on the story or creating their own using toy figures and building blocks.

Time of day: Small-Group Time | **Content area:** Language, Literacy and Communication

Materials

Materials for each child and teacher:
- Small farm animals, 3 of one type
- Small building blocks

Shared materials:
- None

Backup materials:
- Additional assortment of small farm animals

Beginning

- Tell the children that you would like them to help you tell a story similar to "The Three Little Pigs." Say that your story is not about pigs but about three animals of a different kind. Place three animals of one type (e.g., three cows) on the table and begin the story.
- Use the small building blocks to create simple structures to represent each of the three houses in the story.
- Stop the story and give children their own set of three animals and blocks. (You can stop the story after the houses are built or at any point you sense the children are ready to pick it up on their own, for example, after only one or two houses are built or later, after the wolf appears.)
- Suggest the children finish the story or make up a different story using their own animals and blocks.

Middle

- As children use their materials, listen to whether they continue the original story or create their own. Comment on elements of their story that are similar to or different from the original version.
- Repeat the children's words and add new vocabulary words (e.g., *So the big dog barked and the barn fell down*).
- Offer additional animals to children. These can be in sets of three, or children might want to use individual animals or mixed sets.

End

- Tell children that they have time to say/do one more thing in their story.
- Encourage children to put all their blocks and animals back into their containers.
- Suggest that children might want to make animal noises on their way to the next part of the daily routine. Ask them the name of the animal and repeat their choices (e.g., *Noelle is going to make a noise like a parakeet; Sol is going to be a horse*).

Ideas for follow-up

- Read other folktales with children. Retell them together with the children at large-group time, and act out the roles.
- Add farm animals and small blocks to the classroom materials.

Adaptations for children with special needs

- Use large blocks and large farm animals for children with visual and/or small-motor coordination difficulties.

Developmental range: Supporting children at different levels

Earlier ⟶   **Middle** ⟶   **Later** ⟶

Children may

- Make animal sounds as they play with their animal figures or pretend their animals are talking.
- Build with the blocks, then use the animals in combination with the blocks (e.g., build an enclosure and put the animals inside).
- Describe the action of their play (e.g., *The horse knocked over the house*).

Adults can

- Use toy animals to "talk" with children's animals, varying pitch and intonation.
- Use an animal to tell part of the story (e.g., *I'm a little cow that is going to build a house of bricks*).
- Repeat and extend children's vocabulary (e.g., *The horse knocked over the house, and now all the bricks are scattered on the ground*).

Children may

- Assign roles to their animal figures (e.g., momma, bad guy, baby).
- Retell parts of the original story using their own animals.
- Create and describe their own plot (e.g., *The momma is in the house and the daddy is at work*).

Adults can

- Ask children if their activity relates to their story (e.g., *Is there a story that goes with your stacking the blocks?*).
- Acknowledge when children have recreated part(s) of the original story (e.g., *Your goat built a house out of straw, just like one of the little pigs*).
- Use "story language" to describe what animals are doing (e.g., *After the wolf blew the house down, the little cow decided to build another house*).

Children may

- Use storytelling language (e.g., *Once upon a time;* third-person narrative style).
- Use phrases from the original story (e.g., *Little pig, little pig, let me in*).
- Retell two or more parts of the original story in sequence.
- Retell the beginning of the story but make up a different ending.

Adults can

- Comment on similarities and differences in the original story and the story the child is making up.
- Ask to join the child's story, using an animal. Use the third-person narrative voice to make contributions (e.g., *One day a cow decided to stroll up to the pig's house and knock on the door*).
- Comment, *I wonder what will happen next.*

As a follow-up to this activity, teachers can add farm animals and other storytelling props to the classroom.

10 Stirring Alphabet Soup

Children use a magnetic wand to find, collect, match, and name letters hidden in a "soup" tub of rice or sand.

Time of day: Small-Group Time

Content area: Language, Literacy, and Communication

Materials

Materials for each child and teacher:

- Plastic tubs (dish tub, rectangular storage container)
- 10–12 small magnetic letters
- Magnetic wands
- Rice or very dry sand

Shared materials:

- None

Backup materials:

- Cookie trays or other flat items with a metallic surface
- Children's name cards
- Extra letters

Beginning

- Place a tub of rice, in which you have hidden magnetic letters, in front of you. Tell children that it is "alphabet soup" but that the letters have disappeared!
- Stir the rice with the magnet wand and pull out some letters. Ask children to help you identify the letters.
- Give each child a tub of rice with hidden letters and a magnetic wand, and encourage children to stir their "soup" and see what they find.

Middle

- Talk with the children about the letters they find and which ones they recognize and can name. Provide names (when asked) of other letters.
- Refer children to one another to see what others have found, for help naming letters (e.g.,

That letter is in Jessica's name. Maybe she can help you name it).

- After children have had time to search for letters, pass out name cards so they can match the letters they find to those in their names, and offer them metal trays on which to place/arrange the letters they find.
- Add extra letters to children's tubs when needed, noticing if they name the letters as you add them and/or they find them.

End

- Ask children to place letters back in their tubs or place found letters in a separate container you place on table.
- Sing the alphabet song as you clean up and transition to the next activity.

Ideas for follow-up

- Place rice and magnetic letters in the sensory table.
- Put labels with the names of the areas of the room on a metal tray. For planning (or recall) time, give children the first letter of their name and have them place the letter on the tray next to the area of the room where they will play (or played).
- Repeat the activity later in the year, adding other simple word cards that children are familiar with.

Adaptations for children with special needs

- For children with visual or motor impairments, use large magnetic letters.
- For children with visual impairments, provide magnifying glasses to help them see/identify the letters they pull out of the rice or sand.

Developmental range: Supporting children at different levels

Earlier ⟶ **Middle** ⟶ **Later** ⟶

Children may

- Collect the letters and call them *letters* or *ABCs*.
- Use letter names (but not associate them with specific letters).
- Match letters to each other or to letters on their name card.
- Place letters all over the metal tray.

Adults can

- Name letters that they and children are holding.
- Match letters and comment on letter shapes (e.g., *This S looks curvy like a snake*).
- Hold up and identify the first letter in the child's name.
- Line up letters on a metal tray.

Children may

- Identify some letters by name.
- Say that a letter is contained in their name.
- Match magnetic letters to the letters on the name card.
- Place letters in a line on the metal tray and tell adult what it says; ask, *What does it say?*

Adults can

- Spell out their own name using magnetic letters.
- Encourage children to find letters in their own name on a name card.
- Move the first letter of adult's name to the end and say, *Now it doesn't say my name. Something's wrong!*

Children may

- Identify many letters by name.
- Make the sound of a letter they are holding.
- Hold up a letter and say a word that begins with that letter or say a word and identify its initial letter.
- Line up letters on the metal tray to make a word.

Adults can

- Make a simple word on their tray, such as *cat*. Change the first letter to make a new word.
- Ask children to think of words that start with a particular letter.
- Say to children, *I want to spell the word* ball. *I need a letter that makes the /b/ sound.*

This child finds magnetic letters in a tub of rice. To her right is her name card so that she can match the letters she finds to those in her name.

II. Physical Development, Health, and Well-Being

Young children's physical development has two components. One is the capacity to use and move their bodies in ways that are safe and natural. The other is the ability to use objects with skill and confidence. Both types of physical development are purposeful and provide satisfaction to children and the adults who care for them. It is exciting to see children's physical capabilities in action during their preschool years. Having mastered as toddlers the basics of locomotion (moving their bodies from place to place) and coordination (moving their limbs and handling objects with ease), preschoolers can now apply these skills to explore their ever-widening world.

The National Education Goals Panel (Kagan, Moore, & Bredekamp 1995) includes physical development as a dimension of school readiness because of its proven connection to overall mental and social functioning. At the most basic level, normal brain development depends upon children receiving adequate physical care and exercising their bodies in safe and unrestricted environments. Maintaining good health and developing their physical skills provides young children with many benefits in their formative years. Using their bodies to accomplish physical feats and complete tasks is inherently gratifying to them and builds their self-confidence. Physical actions also help infants, toddlers, and preschoolers

Children's physical development involves moving their bodies and learning to use objects with skill and confidence.

learn important cognitive and social concepts. For example, by moving their bodies, children begin to form ideas about space and the objects around them. A child's physical being is also a primary means of communicating with others and forming interpersonal relationships.

The idea that children need to be "taught" how to develop physically may seem odd to parents and educators. We assume physical development happens on its own, provided children receive adequate nutrition and have opportunities to move freely and safely at home, in school, and around their neighborhood. However, physical development is not purely maturational, even in the early years. Professor Stephen Sanders, who developed one of the first preschool movement curricula in the country, says, "Movement programs enhance play, and play provides children with the opportunity to practice movement skills in a variety of contexts. Play alone, however, is not a substitute for helping children develop physical skills.... Some structuring of physical activity is necessary to help children maximize their movement experiences" (Sanders, 2002, p. 31).

Movement education is currently receiving increased national attention because of its potential health benefits. This country has seen an unprecedented rise in childhood obesity, which is in turn associated with increased risk for diabetes, heart disease, high blood pressure, colon cancer, and other health problems in adulthood. The percentage of children identified as overweight has more than doubled in the past 30 years. Along with poor diet, "physical inactivity has contributed to the 100% increase in the prevalence of childhood obesity in the United States since 1980" (Sanders, 2002, p. xiii). By contrast, children who develop basic motor skills and are physically active have a greater chance of participating in daily physical activity as adults. Adult activity, in turn, is associated with better physical health and even with enhanced mental well-being.

Developing and exercising basic physical abilities is also important in its own right. Large and fine motor skills serve multiple functions. Physical coordination is essential to accomplish many, if not most, everyday tasks. In addition, movement is, or should be, inherently pleasurable. The motion of our bodies brings joy, whether we are feeling the freedom of using our muscles or expressing creativity in music and dance. Preschoolers enjoy moving to music in dance-like ways or maneuvering objects through space as they vary the direction and speed of their bodies and/or the things they carry. Such freedom of expression can build young children's personal and social confidence.

Conversely, research shows that children who are less physically adept can have problems in other domains of development (Pica, 1997). They may lack social skills with peers, perhaps because they are perceived by others and/or themselves as clumsy or physical "outsiders." Children's self-confidence as risk-takers may also be adversely affected, with troubling implications for their willingness to tackle challenging academic and social tasks.

As a result, the overall school performance and adjustment of children with undeveloped physical skills may suffer. The self-image that young children form in the early grades — whether positive or negative — can color their experiences for the rest of their school years and carry over into adulthood.

Because of its emphasis on "active participatory learning," the HighScope Curriculum naturally promotes children's physical involvement with the world as central to their early growth and development. In the following small-group times, young children explore using their bodies and moving with objects in increasingly complex ways. For more information on early physical development, see *Round the Circle: Key Experiences in Movement for Young Children* (Weikart, 2000) and the movement activities in *50 Large-Group Activities for Active Learners* (Boisvert & Gainsley, 2006).

References

Boisvert, C., & Gainsley, S. (2006). *50 large-group activities for active learners. Teacher's idea book series.* Ypsilanti, MI: HighScope Press.

Kagan, S. L., Moore, E., & Bredekamp, S. (Eds.). (1995, June). *Reconsidering children's early development and learning: Toward common views and vocabulary.* (Goal 1 Technical Planning Group Report 95–03). Washington, DC: National Education Goals Panel.

Pica, R. (1997, June). Beyond physical development: Why young children need to move. *Young Children, 52*(6), 4–11.

Sanders, S. W. (2002). *Active for life: Developmentally appropriate movement programs for young children.* Washington, DC: National Association for the Education of Young Children.

Weikart, P. S. (2000). *Round the circle: Key experiences in movement for young children* (2nd ed.). Ypsilanti, MI: HighScope Press.

▌▌ Body Letters

Children use their bodies to form letter shapes.

Time of day: Small-Group Time	**Content area:** Physical Development, Health, and Well-Being

Materials

Materials for each child and teacher:

- Three-dimensional letters large enough for children to see and handle (at least 4" to 6") and made of one or more materials (e.g., wooden, foam, or sandpaper letters), one for the initial letter in the child's and teacher's name

Shared materials:

- Additional letters

Beginning

- Meet in your usual small-group space. Tell the children that today you will be moving to the carpet (or wherever you have a large open space in your classroom). Ask them to form a train and "chug" over to the carpet.
- Tell children that today they are going to make body letters.
- Hold up the letter *C*. Ask the children if they can move their arms to make the shape of a *C*. Note how children respond to this idea. Imitate their actions. Now hold up the letter *L*. Ask children how they might use their bodies to form an *L*. Again, watch what children do, commenting on the different ways you see them using their bodies to shape them into "letters."
- Give children a three-dimensional letter representing the first letter of their name; invite them to make that letter with their body. (If a child's initial letter is complicated, such as a *W* or a *K*, you might provide a simpler letter, such as an *O* or *L*.)

Middle

- After children have explored their letter and created their representation of that letter with their body, spread out the other letters in the middle of the floor. Invite children to choose additional letters and "recreate" them with their body.
- As children form their letters, name and comment on the properties of the letters (e.g., straight lines, curves) and the sounds they make (e.g., *That's the letter* C. *It makes the /c/ sound like in car*).

End

- After the children have picked up and put away all the letters, encourage them to make a letter with their arms and to take that "arm letter" with them to the next part of the daily routine.

Ideas for follow-up

- Add the book *Pilobolus: The Human Alphabet* to your book area.
- Try the same activity several weeks later with numerals instead of letters.
- Try the same activity later in the year with geometric shapes.

Adaptations for children with special needs

- If children have a physical disability, be sure to let them know that they can use their arms (or other body parts they can easily move) to create letters. They can also tell an adult (teacher or aide) how they want to move, and the adult can assist children in moving their body in that way; or children can direct the adult to move his/her (the adult's) body to create the letter.
- If children have a cognitive disability, choose simple letters for them to represent (e.g., *O, L, I*), and alternate between a curved letter and a straight letter.

Developmental range: Supporting children at different levels

Earlier ────────▶

Children may
- Bend their bodies into shapes that may or may not match their letter.
- Explore their letter and other letters (e.g., trace their fingers around the edges; hold up two letters next to each other to compare them).

Adults can
- Imitate what children do with their bodies.
- Comment on similarities between the form children make with their body and the shape of their letter (e.g., *I see your legs are straight, just like this side part of the* D).
- Comment on curved or straight parts of children's bodies as compared to the form of the letter (e.g., *Your back is curved, but your legs are straight, just like the letter* D).
- Encourage children to find other letters from their name.

Middle ────────▶

Children may
- Create their letter using certain parts of their body (e.g., their arms or legs).
- Create their letter using their whole body.

Adults can
- Suggest that children might want to create other body letters based on their name.
- Ask children if they can use other parts of their body to create their letter.
- Suggest that children might try lying on the floor to create a letter.

Later ────────▶

Children may
- Use their body to create many letters.
- Name and create many letters, even those not in their name.

Adults can
- Ask children to describe what they did to create their letter.
- Imitate what children do, and then make the same letter in another way. Ask children if they can think of another way to make the same letter.
- Choose more complicated letters and ask them what they might do to make them (e.g., letters like *K, Z,* or *W*).
- Make a body letter and ask children to guess what it is.
- Suggest that children might want to guess which letter another child is making.

Children use their bodies to make the letter L *as their "letter train" turns the corner.*

12 Movement Patterns

Children create patterns of movement, copying the teacher's sequences and creating and describing their own.

Time of day: Small-Group Time

Content area: Physical Development, Health, and Well-Being

Materials

Materials for each child and teacher:
- None

Shared materials:
- None

Backup materials:
- None

Beginning
- Stand with the children in a group (this can be done indoors or outside).
- Begin with a two-part movement (e.g., clap, pat head), and repeat it. Encourage children to copy your movements. After several repetitions, say the pattern aloud, emphasizing the first movement of each repetition (e.g., **clap,** *pat head;* **clap,** *pat head;* **clap,** *pat head*).
- Say something like *We just made a pattern by making the same two movements over and over again. Let's see what other patterns we can make.*

Middle
- Ask children to suggest two movements (e.g., jump and bend). Say and do the movement pattern with the children.
- Continue asking children to suggest two movements until each child who wants a turn has made a suggestion. (Do not require children to take a turn.)
- Use the word *pattern* and related language. Say something like *We're making a pattern because we keep repeating the same two movements. It's a pattern because it repeats over and over again.*
- Say each pattern aloud, using your voice to emphasize the first movement of each repetition (e.g., **jump,** *bend;* **jump,** *bend;* **jump,** *bend*).

End
- Give children a warning before you do the last pattern. Ask them to suggest the number of repetitions.
- Create one more movement pattern to transition to the next activity, saying the pattern aloud as children move to the next location.

Ideas for follow-up
- Use movement patterns at transition times (e.g., to help children settle down when they first assemble for large-group time.
- At large-group time, give the children scarves, paper plates, or other objects to hold and incorporate into their movements (e.g., suggest they alternate waving scarves high and low or holding plates in front and to the sides of their bodies).

Adaptations for children with special needs
- For children with visual limitations, emphasize the pattern repetitions with your voice. Use exaggerated movements that are easy to see (e.g., touch two parts of the body that are far apart, such as the head and knees).
- Encourage children with motor limitations to create patterns with body part(s) they can move easily. Prop children on the floor with pillows so their arms are free to move; children can also incorporate parts of their wheelchair into their patterns (e.g., they can alternate patting their armrests and knees, or wheel forward and backward).

Developmental range: Supporting children at different levels

Earlier ⟶

Children may

- Move in random fashion (e.g., jump, bend, turn, wave, turn).
- Copy the first two steps (*AB*) of a movement created by the teacher or another child but not repeat them to carry out the pattern.
- Copy an *ABAB* movement pattern initiated by the teacher or another child; repeat the pattern at least three times.
- Do two or more movements and ask the teacher if it's a pattern (e.g., bend, clap, bend, turn and say, *Did I make a pattern?*).

Adults can

- Copy the sequences a child makes, whether random or patterned; refer to it as a pattern when it is a pattern.
- Encourage children to copy a pattern; do it together with them.
- Repeat a child's pattern and name the movements; emphasize the beginning of each repetition (e.g., *Jason marched and then wiggled his fingers. Let's repeat those movements in a pattern:* **shake,** *wiggle;* **shake,** *wiggle;* **shake,** *wiggle*); encourage children to move and say the pattern with you.

Middle ⟶

Children may

- Say corresponding words while copying a pattern (e.g., *shake, clap, shake, clap*).
- Create a pattern by tapping in two places at least three times.
- Watch to see if others correctly copy the movement pattern they make; correct mistakes made by others (e.g., *You're not doing it the same way; watch me again*).
- Say they are making a pattern but not say what makes it a pattern (e.g., *I made a pattern. Now you try it!*).
- Copy an *AABB* or *AAB* pattern; repeat the pattern at least three times.

Adults can

- Talk about the idea that patterns repeat the same elements in the same sequence (e.g., *We're waving and stretching over and over again. That's what makes it a pattern*).
- Introduce an *AABB* pattern for the children to copy (e.g., *Now I'm going to move a different way: clap, clap, toe tap, toe tap; clap, clap, toe tap, toe tap; clap, clap, toe tap, toe tap. Try it with me*); encourage children to copy and say the pattern aloud.
- Encourage children to create an *AABB* pattern (e.g., *Let's see if you can make a pattern like mine. I moved one way twice, then another way twice, then back to the first move twice and the second move twice. The same two moves, two times, over and over*).

Later ⟶

Children may

- Identify a movement sequence as a pattern; say what makes a pattern a pattern (e.g., *Here's my pattern. I'm going wiggle, boink, wiggle, boink every time, again and again*).
- Extend someone else's pattern by saying how to move next (e.g., *Now we all clap. In Gina's pattern, we always clap after we march*).
- Create an *AABB* or *AAB* pattern.
- Create a three-element pattern (e.g., *ABCABCABC*).

Adults can

- Create an *AAB* or *ABB* pattern using children's ideas about how to move and encourage children to copy it; say the pattern aloud with the children.
- Stop moving and ask children, *How do I move next?*
- Make a mistake (e.g., wave, bend; wave, bend; wave, wave). If children do not correct you, say *Oops. That doesn't look right. Can you see what I did wrong?*; encourage them to help you "fix" your pattern.
- Create sequences (patterned or random), and ask children whether these sequences are patterns (e.g., jump, clap, clap; jump, clap, jump). Ask them which elements make each a pattern.
- Count the number of pattern repetitions with the children; ask them to say how many times they want to repeat a pattern, and count and repeat that many times with them.

13 Scissors and Play Dough

Children cut, shape, and make marks in play dough using a variety of pattern-edged scissors.

Time of day: Small-Group Time

Content area: Physical Development, Health, and Well-Being

Materials

Materials for each child and teacher:
- Play dough
- 2–3 types of pattern-edged scissors that create different cuts (e.g., straight, serrated, scalloped); scissors designed for children with special needs, such as self-opening and easy-to-grip scissors

Shared materials:
- None

Backup materials:
- Extra scissors
- Butter knives or ice cream pop sticks

Beginning
- Give each child a set of materials and say something like *Here are some different types of scissors and play dough. I wonder what kinds of marks and shapes you can make in your play dough while cutting with these different scissors.*

Middle
- Imitate children's actions with your own set of materials.
- Move from child to child, describing what you see them doing with the materials (e.g., *You are using both hands to cut the play dough; Look at the marks you made with these scissors and with those scissors. I wonder why they are different; What is happening to the play dough when you squeeze it like that with the scissors?*).
- Talk with the children about the patterns each type of scissors makes.
- If children are having trouble holding the scissors, refer them to other children and/or give suggestions about or model ways to hold them (e.g., *Lydia placed two fingers in this hole and her thumb in this hole. Can you try that?; Sometimes I hold my scissors like this*). Encourage children to experiment with ways that are comfortable for them.
- Introduce butter knives or ice cream pop sticks if needed.

End
- Have children put the materials away and wash hands if necessary.
- Encourage children to move "like scissors opening and closing" to the next activity.

Ideas for follow-up
- Use different types of scissors with construction paper or cardstock.
- Use scissors to work with clay.

Adaptations for children with special needs
- Provide scissors designed for children with special needs.
- Encourage children with visual limitations to feel the edges (e.g., smooth, serrated, etc.) made by different types of scissors.

Developmental range: Supporting children at different levels

Earlier →

Children may
- Explore play dough in simple ways (pound, roll, push, pull, poke or stab with scissors).
- Press scissors into the play dough; may use both hands together.
- Make a simple object with play dough and then say what they think it looks like (e.g., *Hey! This looks like a ball!*).

Adults can
- Imitate how children are using materials.
- Acknowledge and describe what they see children doing (e.g., *You are rolling your play dough into a ball; You poked it in the middle with the scissors*).

Depending on their developmental level, children squeeze, shape, cut, and press objects into play dough as they explore its properties and exercise their small muscles.

Middle →

Children may
- Hold play dough in one hand and scissors in the other to make small clips and cuts in the play dough.
- Be intentional with the materials and follow through with their ideas (e.g., say they want to make chocolate chip cookies and cut play dough into small pieces, then place them on top of a round and flat piece of play dough).
- Describe what they are doing and/or making, using one or two details (e.g., *I'm cutting all around the sides*).

Adults can
- Try out their own and children's ideas.
- Describe how children are using the scissors (e.g., *I see that you are putting two fingers and your thumb in the holes of the scissors; Patrick put his pointer finger in one hole and his thumb in the other hole and is cutting with the scissors facing down*).
- Converse with children, responding to comments they make about their discoveries (e.g., *Gregory, you noticed that your snake was long but then got shorter when you cut it in half*).

Later →

Children may
- Use more complex skills in working with the scissors and play dough (e.g., roll out play dough and cut pieces of the same shape or size; cut through thicker pieces of play dough with scissors).
- Use scissors to accomplish a plan (e.g., cut into play dough to make ridges for a fence; cut pieces of play dough to mold a figure).
- Describe what they are doing and/or making with three or more details (e.g., *I have to push it flat and cut it down the middle, then I roll this part and smoosh it on top of the other*).

Adults can
- Discuss with children their ideas for using the scissors and play dough (e.g., *I am wondering how you will use the scissors to make teeth for your shark; I wonder what kind of marks you can make with your scissors to make them look like grass*).
- Discuss with children the details of what they are making (or made) by asking open-ended questions (e.g., *I wonder how you made this shape when you used the scissors*).

14 Squeezing at the Water Table

Children use squeezable items to fill and empty cups and containers with water.

Time of day: Small-Group Time

Content area: Physical Development, Health, and Well-Being

Materials

Materials for each child and teacher:

- 1–2 squeezable objects (e.g., turkey baster, sponge)
- 1–2 containers
- 1–2 wide-brimmed cups
- Smock

Shared materials:

- Water table filled with water (additionally, use water basins and the sink in your classroom to allow room for every child)
- Food coloring (optional)

Backup materials:

- "Magic" towels (compressed towels that expand in water)
- Extra containers
- Extra items to squeeze (e.g., a variety of sponges of different shapes and sizes; small plastic pipettes; rubber squeeze bulbs; small easy-squeeze bottles, such as ketchup or mustard containers)

Beginning

- Announce that today for small-group time you will move over to the water table (or sink, etc.).
- Say something like *Today we are going to squeeze water from sponges, bottles, and other squeezable things. I wonder how we might use our hands to squeeze water from these things.*

Middle

- Make descriptive comments about what children are doing. Encourage them to describe their motions. Repeat their words and introduce new vocabulary words related to squeezing, opening and closing hands, filling and emptying, and so on.
- Ask children to squeeze out all the water from the magic towels to make them small again.

End

- Have children do one last squeeze and put the materials in designated containers for storage. Let them know the sponges and other items will be available at work time.
- Ask children to squeeze their arms close to their sides as they move to the next activity.

Ideas for follow-up

- At another small-group time, repeat the activity but let each child have his or her own sponges and individual pans of water.
- At outside time, fill a galvanized tub, basins, plastic buckets, and other containers with water. Bring out a variety of items the children can use to fill and squeeze.
- Together with the children, wash outdoor equipment (e.g., bikes, slide, swings) using buckets of water and squeezable materials.
- Encourage children to explore squeezing other items and materials (e.g., clay and play dough; rolled towels; bundles of fabric; dry, wadded, or wet newspaper).

Adaptations for children with special needs

- For children with muscle limitations, include items that can be easily squeezed (e.g., thin plastic squeeze bottles, sponges with less density).

Developmental range: Supporting children at different levels

Earlier ⟶

Middle ⟶

Later ⟶

Children may

- Use their cup as a scoop to fill a container.
- Pour water from one container to another.
- Try to get water in the turkey baster without squeezing the bulb.
- Squeeze the water out of sponges to fill a container.

Adults can

- Comment on what they see children doing (e.g., *You are scooping the water and filling the yogurt container*).
- Model how to use the turkey baster. Use two hands to squeeze the bulb. Note to children that they have to squeeze really hard to fill it with water.
- Refer children to one another for assistance (e.g., comment that another child is using a squeeze bulb to fill a container).
- Acknowledge children's efforts and actions (e.g., *You squeezed the sponge with all your might to get the water into the pail!*).

Children may

- Fill multiple containers with water using all the materials.
- After squeezing a bottle upright, get excited about seeing the water squirt straight up in the air (e.g., *Wow! I made a fountain!*).
- Describe their actions, (e.g., *I used both hands and squeezed really, really hard*).

Adults can

- Ask children how many cups they've filled; help them count, modeling one-to-one correspondence (e.g., pointing to or moving each cup in the process of counting).
- Comment about the different tools used to fill the cups. Ask children which tools they prefer and why.
- Comment to children that different tools require more/less pressure (e.g., *With some tools you use your whole hand to squeeze and get water and with other tools you only use your fingertips and thumbs*).

Children may

- Experiment with the turkey baster until they find a technique that works for them (e.g., *If you keep the tip in the water and squeeze hard, you get the mostest water*).
- Compare squeezers or containers and say which holds more/most (e.g., *You can get more water in the cup with the bottle than with the sponge*).
- Make a game with another child to see who can fill a cup faster.

Adults can

- Challenge children to guess (estimate) how many times they have to squeeze a sponge to fill a cup or a bowl with water. Ask children if they think it would take the same number of times with another tool.
- Ask children to describe what they will do to be the "fastest" one to fill a container with water.
- Use and encourage children to use words related to their actions (e.g., *squeezing, filling, emptying*) and words that describe the results they observe (e.g., *half-full, overflowing*).

As they squeeze bottles and other items, children practice motor skills and eye-hand coordination; they also learn about measurement and spatial concepts.

15 Treetops Moving in the Wind

Children move the upper parts of their bodies while standing in place, imitating the movement of trees in the wind. [Note: You might do this activity the day after you and the children have noticed the wind in the trees during outside time.]

Time of day: Small-Group Time

Content area: Physical Development, Health, and Well-Being

Materials

Materials for each child and teacher:
• Carpet squares or circles for children to stand on

Shared materials:
• None

Backup materials:
• Instrumental music

Beginning

• Announce that today for small-group time you will move to an area where children can have their own space to move in various ways. When everyone is gathered, ask children to find a space of their own on a carpet square or circle.

• Say something like *I wonder how our bodies would move if we were a tree planted in the ground and we could only move our upper part, like the branches and leaves.* Demonstrate moving only your upper body while standing in place. Then add *How would we move our tops if a big gust of wind came by and blew at us? What if a tiny breeze came by and blew our treetops? How would we move then?*

Middle

• Watch how children move and make descriptive comments on what they are doing with their bodies and body parts. Remind them that their roots are firmly planted in the ground and only the tops of their trees can move.

• Imitate children's actions; encourage them to describe what they are doing so you can do the same thing.

• Ask children who want to be the leader to take turns, and have other children imitate their movements. If necessary, help leaders demonstrate or describe their movements.

• Ask who wants to lead the group in moving their trees to the music. After everyone who wants to lead has a turn, put on the music. Encourage children to move their treetops to the music.

End

• Tell the children that this is the last tree movement and that this time they will pretend they are trees that can walk. Ask them to move to the next part of the daily routine as a "walking tree."

Ideas for follow-up

• During outside time or large-group time, play follow the leader with children, moving in non-locomotor (moving in place) and/or locomotor ways (moving from one place to another).

Adaptations for children with special needs

• This activity is good for children with mobility difficulties because they can use their upper bodies. Encourage them to incorporate their assistive devices in their movements (e.g., by rotating the wheels of their wheelchair back and forth).

• If children have difficulty moving their upper bodies, encourage them to move their legs, their heads, or any other body part they can move. Let them be the leader (if they volunteer), and encourage other children to copy their movements.

Developmental range: Supporting children at different levels

Earlier ⟶

Children may
- Move their entire body instead of just the upper part.
- Move the upper part of their body in one or two ways.
- Copy what the person next to them is doing.
- Follow the leader's simple (one step) movements (e.g., watch and copy the teacher or another child swing his/her arms back and forth).
- Continue the previous movement or begin another movement that is not the same as the leader's.
- Follow the leader's example halfway through the turn.

Adults can
- Comment on or describe children's movements; wonder what children would do if they could only move upper body (e.g., *You're jumping up and down. Suppose you were planted in the ground and the wind blew you from here up* [point from your waist up to your head]. *How would you move then?*).
- Attach a verbal label to the children's actions before copying it (e.g., watch a child move his/her arms, say *you're swinging,* and move your arms in the same way).
- After each turn, draw the children's attention to the new leader (e.g., shake a bell and say *Time for a new leader. Kelly, would you like to choose a way to move?*).

Middle ⟶

Children may
- Move the upper part of their body in three or more ways.
- Follow the leader's example and then change it in some way (e.g., swing arms by their side like the leader and then swing them back and forth together in front of their body).
- Follow the leader's complex (two or more steps) movements (e.g., watch and copy the leader alternate tapping his/her head and shoulder; twist in one direction and then another).

Adults can
- Comment on the different ways children move (e.g., *First your treetop waved its arms, then it shook its head, and now its shoulders are going up and down, up and down*).
- Acknowledge children's additions (e.g., *Henry found a different way to swing his arms. Let's try it Henry's way*).
- Offer nonverbal support to the followers (e.g., smile, nod your head, look interested, match the speed and rhythm of your movements to theirs).

Later ⟶

Children may
- Initiate (lead) a complex movement involving two or more steps (e.g., touch head then knees and say, *This is a tricky one!*).
- Describe or name their idea and then demonstrate the action (e.g., say *punch,* and punch a fist into the air).
- Comment on which part(s) of their body they are moving and which part(s) they are keeping still (e.g., *I'm moving my arms but not my feet. They're stuck in the ground!*).

Adults can
- Attach labels to children's actions; encourage children to name their actions (e.g., *What do you call it when you go like this?*).
- Acknowledge when children create a two-step (or more complex) movement (e.g., *You made your tree move in two ways. You're swinging both arms and then tapping your head, swinging and tapping*).
- Ask children questions about the rate of movement (e.g., *Should we punch fast or slow?*).
- Ask children to say which body part(s) to move and which to keep still in order to copy their movements.

III. Mathematics

In the past 25 years, researchers have come to appreciate how much young children enjoy and are capable of mathematical investigation and reasoning. For example, when Herbert Ginsburg and his colleagues observed children's free play, they were amazed not only by how much children used mathematical ideas, but also by the advanced level of their thinking (Ginsburg, Inou, & Seo, 1999). Professor Arthur Baroody (2000) says preschoolers actively construct basic mathematical concepts and use them to solve problems. Young children do not merely "receive" such knowledge, they build it from experience. This is why it is so important for preschoolers to engage in activities that allow them to work with materials, pursue their own investigations, and draw conclusions, with thoughtful *What if …?*-type questions from adults.

The field has further discovered that early mathematics learning involves more than simply reciting numerals or counting by rote. It also includes investigations into patterns, size and quantity, and spatial relations — the building blocks for more advanced concepts in algebra, measurement, and geometry, respectively. The standards of the National Council of Teachers of Mathematics (NCTM, 2000) list five content areas for mathematics learning, the first three (called "focal points") being especially important in the early childhood years (NCTM, 2006):

- **Number and operations** involves understanding whole numbers and realizing that numbers represent quantity. It includes learning number words and symbols, counting, comparing and ordering quantities, composing (combining) and decomposing (dividing) numbers, and simple addition and subtraction.
- **Geometry** involves identifying shapes and describing spatial relationships and includes learning the names and properties of two- and three-dimensional shapes; transformation (changing shapes, putting them together and taking them apart); and spatial reasoning (using position, direction, and distance words).
- **Measurement** involves identifying measurable attributes and using them to compare objects, actions, people, and events. For young children, this means learning simple measurement terms and processes, understanding what a "unit" is, and comparing and ordering attributes.
- **Algebra** involves identifying patterns and relationships, including describing, copying, and creating simple alternating patterns (e.g., *ABABAB, ABCABCABC, AABAABAAB*) and recognizing and describing increasing and decreasing patterns (such as cycles of plant growth or the change of seasons).
- **Data analysis** involves formulating and answering questions by collecting, organizing, and analyzing information. In the early years this includes describing attributes, organizing and comparing simple data, representing findings

Children's investigations into patterns, size, quantity, and spatial relations lay the foundation for more advanced concepts in math.

on simple charts or graphs, and interpreting and applying the lessons learned.

In young children, we can see early mathematics curiosity, investigation, and development in a variety of situations. Math learning is taking place whenever children are engaged in the following activities:

- *Observing* — discovering and creating knowledge about the world using all of one's senses (for example, seeing colors ranging from light to dark; hearing sounds that vary in pitch and loudness)
- *Exploring materials* — discovering the properties of objects and how things work; seeing how things change when they are acted upon by people or events (for example, seeing what happens when two colors of paint are mixed together; observing what happens on the screen after hitting different computer keys)
- *Working with numbers* — intuiting amounts (pre-counting); understanding that numerals represent numbers of objects; grasping one-to-one correspondence; counting; knowing that the quantity stays the same even if the shape of the container or arrangement of objects changes (conservation)
- *Ordering* — putting objects and people in a graduated order based on an attribute on which they differ (e.g., size, age, loudness, color intensity, speed, pitch)
- *Navigating space* — arranging objects; understanding how one's body relates to the objects and spaces around it; fitting things together and taking them apart; understanding direction and position concepts
- *Comparing quantities* — recognizing relative size and amounts (e.g., bigger/smaller, more/less); comparing amounts in continuous materials (e.g., sand and water) and discrete objects (e.g., blocks and beads)
- *Identifying regularities* — recognizing, copying, adding to, and creating patterns; identifying regularity and repetition in objects and events; making predictions based on observed patterns
- *Classifying* — organizing and sorting information; fitting new information into existing categories or changing categories to fit the new

information (for example, moving from calling all four-legged pets "dogs" to differentiating between dogs and cats; distinguishing living and nonliving things)
- *Drawing conclusions* — offering explanations of what one observes; predicting — accurately or not — what will happen (for example, deciding the cat likes wet food more than dry food because it eats more of it; guessing someone is older because they are taller)
- *Communicating ideas* — sharing one's thoughts about the world with others through talking, drawing, writing, or other means of representation (for example, giving directions to a peer on how to build a tall block tower that will not fall down; sharing information about how to get a computer program to work)

The small-group activities that follow are designed so that preschoolers can construct mathematical knowledge by manipulating materials and ideas in all of these ways. For further ideas to support young children's learning in this content area, see the teacher idea book *I'm Older Than You. I'm Five! Math in the Preschool Classroom* (Epstein & Gainsley, 2005), and *Numbers Plus Preschool Mathematics Curriculum* (HighScope, 2009).

References

Baroody, A. J. (2000, July). Does mathematics instruction for three- to five-year olds really make sense? *Young Children, 55*(4), 61–67.

Epstein, A. S., & Gainsley, S. (2005). *I'm older than you. I'm five! Math in the preschool classroom.* Ypsilanti, MI: HighScope Press.

Ginsburg, H. P., Inoue, N., & Seo, K. H. (1999). Young children doing mathematics: Observations of everyday activities. In J. V. Copley (Ed.), *Mathematics in the early years.* Reston, VA: National Council of Teachers of Mathematics and National Association for the Education of Young Children, 88–99.

HighScope Educational Research Foundation. (2009). *Numbers Plus Preschool Mathematics Curriculum.* Ypsilanti, MI: HighScope Press.

National Council of Teachers of Mathematics. (2000). *Principles and standards for school mathematics.* Reston, VA: Author.

National Council of Teachers of Mathematics. (2006). *Curriculum focal points for prekindergarten through grade 8 mathematics: A quest for coherence.* Reston, VA: Author.

16 Basket Toss

Children throw tossable items into large baskets, counting and comparing baskets they make or miss.

Time of day: Small-Group Time   **Content area:** Mathematics

Materials

Materials for each child and teacher:

- 5 beanbags or other tossable items (e.g., foam balls; small paper or plastic bags filled with beans/coins and taped shut; small balls made from crumpled newspaper)
- Small container to hold the beanbags
- Large container (e.g., basket, bucket, or trash can)
- 1 piece of chart paper, labeled with each child's name, letter link, or symbol; make one column for each "game," and label them 1, 2, 3 (for first, second, third, etc.), up to five games

Shared materials:

- None

Backup materials:

- None

Beginning

- Talk to the children about their experiences playing or watching basketball. Say *Today we're going to shoot some baskets with beanbags* (or whichever object is being tossed into the basket).
- Model how to play the game. Stand about three feet away from a large container and toss your five beanbags one at a time toward the basket. Count each shot aloud, saying *one, two, three, four, five.* Try to make a few shots and miss a few shots. Together with the children, count the number of shots you made and the number of shots you missed. Write the number of shots you made in the appropriate column/row on the chart. Use dots or dash marks (one mark for each basket made) and numerals. Collect your beanbags for another game.

- Distribute the beanbags or other tossable items to each child. Spread out the large containers with enough room between them so that children have space to throw freely. Say *Let's see how many baskets you can shoot.*

Middle

- Do not be concerned if children don't stand exactly three feet away from the large basket or follow other "rules." Focus on the mathematics learning.
- Each time children shoot a set of five beanbags, ask them to count the number of baskets they made and to record it (with your help if needed) on their chart, using tally marks or numerals. (You don't need to record every game for every child, as long as each child has several scores).
- Take an occasional turn yourself and enter your scores on your chart.
- When children have several scores, ask them to indicate the highest/lowest number of baskets they made (or the game in which they made the most/fewest baskets). Encourage them to compare their chart to others' (yours or those of their peers) to find scores that are higher/lower than their own (or games with more/fewer baskets made). Ask them to indicate if they scored higher/lower (or made more/fewer baskets than you did) in the first game, second game, and so on. Point to and label corresponding columns (e.g., first, second, etc.).

End

- Bring the activity to a close by saying something like *Wow! We made a lot of baskets today. Let's look at our score sheets and count how many.* Talk to the children about the tally marks on their charts, helping them to count the marks and write the total number of baskets scored at the bottom of their page.

- Together with the children, gather the materials and put them away. Remind them they can play basket toss at work/choice time. Choose a place to store the charts in case children want to continue keeping track of their scores.

- Use the children's scores and the order of the games to transition to the next activity. Say, for example, *Whoever shot a 3 on their last game, go to the snack table. Whoever shot a 2 on their first game, go to the snack table next,* until all the children have made the transition.

Ideas for follow-up

- Play basket toss with a larger number of beanbags (up to 10).

- Vary the distance from the basket, and ask children to compare how many baskets they make from different distances. Use terms like *closer/ nearer/farther* for distances and *more/fewer/ same* for the number of baskets made.

- For planning or recall, place an area sign on each container, and ask children to toss a ball into the container labeled with the name of the area where they'd like to work (or did work).

Adaptations for children with special needs

- Adjust (shorten) the throwing distance for children with limited vision or mobility.

- Help children with limited mobility retrieve beanbags and/or encourage their peers to help them.

Developmental range: Supporting children at different levels

Earlier ⟶ **Middle** ⟶ **Later** ⟶

Children may

- Use descriptive language to talk about the number of beanbags (e.g., *I scored a lot*).
- Say numerals aloud but not connect counting to the number of beanbags inside/outside their container.
- Count but not use the last number counted to determine the total quantity (e.g., *One, two, three. I got five*).
- Refer to more than two or three items as a "big number"; may state a number they perceive as big (e.g., *five, one hundred, a gazillion*).
- Make a nonrepresentative mark or tally on the chart (e.g., single line or scribble).

Adults can

- Count together with child, pointing at each beanbag and saying the number.
- After child counts, say *How many is that?*
- Repeat the last number counted as the total number (quantity) of beanbags (e.g., *One, two, three. You made three baskets*).
- Help child make a representative number of tally marks on the chart. Say *You made one, two, three baskets,* and make a corresponding mark for each number.
- Stack or line up containers so the children can visually compare the number of beanbags inside the containers. Ask children, *Which has more (fewer)? Are they the same?*

Children may

- Estimate (without counting) the number of beanbags inside/outside their container.
- Count the number of beanbags but not necessarily correctly (may skip or duplicate numbers).
- Count and use the last number to state their score (e.g., *One, two, three, four. I scored four baskets*).
- Compare the number of baskets made nonnumerically (e.g., *I scored more than you*).
- State the number in two different scores/sets without comparing them (e.g., *I got five and you got three*).
- Record the number of baskets on the chart with representative tally marks but not necessarily correctly (may score five but make four tally marks).

Adults can

- Ask children who make estimates, *How can you tell you made three baskets? How do you know I made two and you made four?*
- Ask, *How do you know you scored more/fewer baskets than I did?*
- Encourage numerical comparisons (e.g., *You said you had five and I got three. So who made more baskets?*).
- Model strategies for keeping track while counting (e.g., move object to a different pile after it has been counted).
- Count tally marks with children. Ask them if the number of marks is the same as their score. Encourage children to do one-to-one correspondence to compare.

Children may

- Correctly count the number of beanbags inside/outside their container.
- Count to compare the number of beanbags in two containers and state which has more/fewer (e.g., *I got five and you got three. You don't have as many as me*).
- Compare the numbers in two different score sets, stating which has more/fewer (e.g., *You got three more baskets than me this time*).
- Compare and order three or more scores (e.g., *I got 5, 3, and then 2. That's the most [points to 5], that's the smallest [points to 2], and this is in the middle [points to 3]*).
- Use numerals to record the number of baskets made but not necessarily correctly (may score two baskets but write a 3); ask how to write a specific numeral (e.g., *How do you make a four?*).

Adults can

- Ask, *How many more/fewer baskets did you make than me?*
- Suggest strategies to help children compare quantity (e.g., *If you stacked your beanbags after each game, which pile would be higher?*).
- Look at child's chart and ask, *In which game did you score the most? In which did you score the fewest?* If child points, say *That's the first game where you scored the most,* and so on.
- Encourage child to order three or more games. Ask, *Which score is the highest? lowest? in between?; Which game has the most/fewest baskets? Which has the second most/fewest?*
- Match tally marks to numerals (e.g., *You made three dots. We write 3 like this*).

17 Flip-and-Turn Worms

Children play with blocks to explore how a shape remains the same even when its position or orientation is changed by flipping it over or turning it. Then children flip and turn their own bodies.

Time of day: Small-Group Time

Content Area: Mathematics

Materials

Materials for each child and teacher:

- 5–10 small, flat, elongated objects such as wooden blocks, Duplos, or Legos that can also stand on end

Shared materials:

- None

Backup materials:

- None

Beginning

- Talk to the children about what it means to flip or turn something. Ask them to think of things that can be flipped (such as pancakes) or turned (i.e., rotated, such as the pieces of a puzzle).
- Say *These are called flip-and-turn-worms. They move by making flips and turns.* Model and label movements of the flip-and-turn worms. Say *These are flips* (turn flat worm face up and face down, then flip over end to end; turn standing worm on end with top up and top down, then flip (side to side); then say *these are turns* (rotate worm fully and partially, oriented flat or on end). Use position and direction words to describe the movements and the orientations of the worms (right-side up and upside down, forwards and backwards, end over end, sideways, and so on).
- Distribute the "worms," and say something like *I wonder how you will make your worms flip over and turn.*

Middle

- Circulate among the children, describing and discussing the flips and turns they make with their worms.
- Midway through the activity, encourage children to lie on the floor and flip and turn their own bodies. For example, they may lie face down and flip over to lie face up. They can flip just their palms from face up to face down. Or they may lie on their backs with their heads close to the table and their feet pointing toward the middle of the room, then turn (rotate) so their feet are close to the table and their heads point toward the middle of the room.

End

- Together with the children, sort and put away the materials.
- Remind children that the materials will be available during work/choice time should they want to use them.
- Encourage children to flip and/or turn their bodies to transition to the next activity.

Ideas for follow-up

- At large-group time, do flip-and-turn movements with the children. Encourage them to describe (label) their movements. Have them take turns being leaders and doing flip and/or turn movements for other children to copy.
- At planning (or recall) time, have children flip or turn a block to point to the area of the classroom where they will play (or played).

- At a small- or large-group outside time, have children flip or turn toward a bush, bench, or similar marker. For example, if children are lying on their backs and looking up at the sky, you might say, *I wonder how the clouds would look if we turned our bodies so our heads were next to the bush and our feet were pointed toward the swings.* If children go down the slide on their backs, you might challenge them to "flip over" and slide down on their stomachs, but always feet first.
- Tape an outline on the floor (such as a rectangle or circle) and ask the children to be flip-and-turn worms going *into* the space, *out* of the space, to the *other side,* and so on. Label and encourage children to label and describe the type and direction of their movements.

- Provide other objects children can flip and turn (e.g., puzzle pieces, dominoes, playing cards, felt shapes). Discuss whether these objects look the same/different after flips and turns.

Adaptations for children with special needs

- Children can work on wheelchair trays instead of at the table or on the floor.
- Use larger blocks ("worms") for children who have difficulty grasping/manipulating smaller blocks.
- Children who cannot flip and turn their whole bodies can be encouraged to flip and turn part(s) of their bodies, such as a hand or arm. They can also use a doll or stuffed animal in place of their own bodies.

Adults use position and direction words to describe the movements and orientations of children's flip-and-turn "worms."

Developmental range: Supporting children at different levels

Earlier ⟶

Middle ⟶

Later ⟶

Children may
- Move worms in other ways (e.g., spins, slides, hops, jumps); label some or all of these other movements correctly and/or call them flips and turns.
- Be unable to move their own bodies in flips and turns.

Adults can
- Acknowledge and imitate movements children make, challenging them to try other ways (e.g., *You hopped your worm. I wonder if you can flip it like this*).
- Refer children to one another, and encourage them to comment on flips and turns made by peers.
- Label and describe other movements the children make with their worms; label and describe how these movements differ from flips and turns.
- Lie down and demonstrate flips and turns for children. Physically assist children in making flips and turns.

Children may
- Do flips or turns, but not both, with worms.
- Correctly label flips or turns, but not both, with worms (e.g., call everything a flip or turn, reverse labels).
- Do flips and/or turns with worms in one orientation (flat or on end).
- Do flips and/or turns with worms but not with their own bodies.
- Correctly label flips and/or turns with worms but not in relation to their own bodies.

Adults can
- Label and describe flips and turns with worms, emphasizing how the movements differ. Use terms such as *this side, the other side, end over end,* and so on, to help differentiate the two movements.
- Encourage children to do flips and turns with their bodies. Talk about how children's body movements parallel the worm movements.
- Model doing flips and turns with worms in different orientations (e.g., flat or on end). Describe and talk about how the basic movement is the same, regardless of the initial orientation.
- Make different worm or body movements, and encourage children to label and describe them.

Children may
- Do flips and turns with worms and correctly label each movement.
- Do flips and/or turns with worms in more than one orientation (flat and on end).
- Do flips and/or turns with both worms and their own bodies.
- Correctly label (differentiate) flips and turns.
- Correctly label (differentiate) other types of movements with worms and/or bodies (e.g., slides, spins)

Adults can
- Encourage children to describe their worm and body movements made in different orientations (e.g., flat, on end).
- Introduce other vocabulary words for flips and turns (e.g., *somersault, end over end, backflip*).
- Model and label other worm and body movements (e.g., spinning, rolling, and zigzagging).
- Encourage children to describe the direction and orientation of their worms' flips and turns (e.g., flipping to the bottom edge of the table, turning like a clock).

18 Going Shopping

Children go to the "store" to buy a number of items corresponding in quantity to a number they roll on a die.

Time of day: Small-Group Time   **Content area:** Mathematics

Materials

Materials for each child and teacher:

- Basket, shopping bag, or other container large enough to hold at least 20 small items
- 1 die

Shared materials:

- Assortment of 5–6 types of small items such as plastic animals, buttons, beans, and straws; 50 or more of each item arranged as a "store" (e.g., in bins on the small-group table, in baskets in the house area, on tables in the hallway)

Backup materials:

- Additional items to stock the store

Beginning

- Tell the children they are going shopping for presents. Talk about when they might buy presents (e.g., birthdays and holidays) and where they would go to shop for them.
- Show them the "store" in the classroom. Together with the children, name and talk about the items available at the store. (Children may also want to give the store a name.)
- Model "going shopping." Roll your die, point to and count the number of dots you roll, saying *I rolled a five, so I get to shop for five items. All the items can be the same, like five beads, or I can get different items as long as they add up to five. I think I will go shopping and buy four bears and one bead.* Choose and count out five items and place them in your container.
- Give each child a die and a container. Tell the children to roll their die, determine the number of dots, and go to the store to buy the given number of items. You might say something like *I wonder what number you'll roll and which items you'll choose at the store.*

Middle

- Tell the children they can keep shopping until the store is out of goods.
- Help children count the number of dots they roll on the die and the corresponding number of items from the store. After each shopping trip, ask children if they bought *more, fewer,* or the *same* number of items as you.

End

- Tell the children it's time for the store to close. Together with the children, return the items to their regular storage places, and decide where to keep the bins/baskets should children want to set up a store at work/choice time.
- Transition to the next activity based on items children bought (e.g., *Whoever bought bears, go to the snack table; Anyone who bought crayons can go next;* etc.), until all the children have moved to the next activity.

Ideas for follow-up

- If you see children playing store at work/choice time, model using the die to decide how many things to purchase. Watch to see if they incorporate this idea into their play.
- At planning (or recall) time, ask each child to roll a die and to share the corresponding number of ideas about his or her plan (or recall). You might say, for example, *Elayna, you rolled a two. Can you tell me two things about your plan?* Or, *Carl, you counted one dot. What's one thing you played with at work (choice) time?* (If children make fewer or more statements about their plan/recall, accept their response, but relate what they say back to the number on the die, for example, *Carl told us he played with the dishes. That's one thing. He also said he played with the water, so that's two things*).

Adaptations for children with special needs

- Children who have trouble rolling the die can choose a dot on the die, pick a number card out of a bag, or point to one of a set of cards turned faced down, for example, to determine the number of items they will shop for on each turn.
- Encourage children with visual disabilities to roll the die, then set out a number of small objects (such as counting bears) that corresponds to the number they rolled. Help the child feel and count each object, using one-to-one correspondence. You can also make a large die from a wooden cube, drilling holes (one through six) in each side that children can feel with their fingers.
- Include items in the store that children with visual disabilities can feel, smell, or hear.
- Help children with limited mobility retrieve items from the store and/or encourage other children to help them "go shopping."

Children roll the die, determine the number of dots, and then go "shopping" to buy the corresponding number of items at the "store."

Developmental range: Supporting children at different levels

Earlier →

Children may

- Roll die but not count dots.
- Not connect or associate the number of items they shop for with the number on the die.
- Gesture or describe the items in their basket nonnumerically (e.g., *I got a lot of stuff; Look! I have a teeny bunch of beads*).
- Say numbers aloud but not connect them to the act of counting; count numbers by rote without reference to dots or items.
- State a number of dots or items at random without attempting to count them (e.g., *I bought ten bears; I got a thousand straws*).
- Compare collections nonnumerically (e.g., *Mine are bigger; You bought more/less*).

Adults can

- Emphasize counting using one-to-one correspondence, pointing to or touching each dot and item as it is counted.
- If children point to their collection, ask, *How many is that?*
- Support children's statements about bigness (e.g., *Yes, one hundred is a big number. Let's count to see the big number of things you bought at the store*).
- Encourage children to sort their sets into small piles and count the number of items in each.

Middle →

Children may

- State the number of dots or items by eyeballing small numbers rather than counting (up to three–five).
- Count the number of dots or items but not necessarily correctly (count out of order, skip, and/or duplicate).
- Count a collection but not use the last number to determine quantity (e.g., *One, two, three. I got five*).
- Count the dots but do not correctly match the number to the number of items (e.g., count four dots but choose five items).
- Compare two sets of items, aligning them to see which has more (e.g., *My line of bears is longer than my line of shells. I bought more bears*).

Adults can

- Model strategies for keeping track while counting (e.g., move counted objects to the side; make a row or column before counting).
- Emphasize that the last number counted is the total quantity in the set (e.g., *One, two, three. You bought three bears at the store*).
- Encourage children to count and state the number of items in their set. After children finish counting, ask, *So, how many is that?*
- Model strategies for comparing quantities. Create a set of items much larger than the child's. Ask child to count both sets and say, *Which set took longer to count?* Connect the longer counting time with the higher/larger number.
- Ask, *Who has more (or fewer)? How can you tell?* Encourage child to count and state how many items are in each set. Then ask, *So who has more?*

Later →

Children may

- Count correctly the number of dots or items using one-to-one correspondence (may point to or move each as it is counted).
- Use the last number counted to state how many there are in the total set (e.g., *One, two, three, four. I have four bears*).
- Count the number of items in two sets by counting them and stating the results numerically but not say which one has more/fewer than the other (e.g., *One, two, three. One, two, three, four. You have three and I have four*).
- Compare the number of items in two sets using words such as *more/fewer, smaller/bigger,* and *same* (e.g., *One, two, three. One, two, three, four, five. This one* [pointing at set of five] *has more*).

Adults can

- Miscount the number of items in a set and see if the child corrects the mistake. If not, recount the set and state a different number. Say, *Something is wrong. First I counted four, now I counted five. Can you help me count?*
- Ask children to count how many of each item are left in the store. Note if there are "zero" left.
- Ask which item has the most, fewest, or same amount left in the store.
- Ask children how many more/fewer items one set has compared to another; ask them to share their strategies for determining which set has more/fewer.
- Order three collections in a row and ask children where one or more other collections belong in the row (e.g., order collections of two, four, and five items, and ask where the set of one and/or three belong).

19 How Much Does It Hold?

Children count how many turkey basters full of water it takes to fill a cup. (This activity can also be done as an outside small-group time or at the water table.)

Time of day: Small-Group Time

Content Area: Mathematics

Materials

Materials for each child and teacher:
- Turkey baster
- Tubs filled with water (e.g., empty toy bins, dish tubs)
- Plastic cups (e.g., 12 or 16 ounces)
- Paper and markers for recording (tallying) measurements
- Smock

Shared materials:
- Plastic tablecloths or drop cloths
- Sponges

Backup materials:
- Cups or other containers in additional sizes (ranging from 4–32 ounces)

Beginning

- Hold up a cup and say *I wonder how to measure how much water this cup can hold.* Ask children for suggestions, and try out their ideas.
- Suggest using a turkey baster. Model filling a turkey baster completely full with water from the washtub and squirting it into the cup. Say *That's one turkey baster full of water,* and record one tally mark on a piece of paper. Repeat this process until the cup is full, counting aloud and recording each basterful. When the cup is full, repeat how many basters filled with water were used, for example, *This cup holds three turkey basters of water.*
- Distribute one turkey baster and a cup to each child. Say *Let's see if you can measure how much water this cup can hold.*

Middle

- Assist children who are having trouble filling the turkey baster. Model again how to use it, referring children to one another for help. Do not be concerned if children cannot fill the baster all the way, as long they grasp the idea of repeating the same procedure each time.
- Encourage children to use the turkey basters to measure how much water each cup holds (volume). Discuss the different sizes of cups, from smallest to biggest (and vice versa), and compare how many basters full of water each cup holds.
- Help children count and record their measurements. Encourage them to make tally marks, or write the tally marks for them. For children who are ready to compare the volume of different-sized cups, help them divide a sheet of paper into columns (corresponding to the different cup sizes) and/or to use a different sheet of paper for each cup size.
- Midway through the activity, introduce cups of other sizes. Encourage children to compare the amount of water different cups hold.

End

- Share and discuss as a group the children's measurements of volume for different-sized cups.
- Together with the children, empty the water from the cups into the tubs. Remind children where they can find the cups and basters should they want to use them again at work/ choice time.
- Encourage children to guess how many steps it will take them to get to the next activity.

Ideas for follow-up

- Measure the volume of other containers of different sizes (e.g., plastic food containers, jugs cut to different heights, aluminum cans).
- Measure volume using other nonstandard units (e.g., eyedroppers, sponges) as well as standard units (e.g., measuring cups, spoons).
- Measure the volume of containers using other fillers (e.g., sand, pebbles, shells, dried beans).

Adaptations for children with special needs

- Children who cannot grasp or squeeze the turkey baster may be able to pour water from smaller cups into the tub. They can also give squeezing or pouring directions to the teacher (or another child) to carry out for them.
- Children with visual limitations can feel how much space there is between the water level and the top of the tub each time they add another baster or cup full of water. Align cups of different sizes next to one another so children can feel their graduated heights.

Teachers encourage children to measure how much water their turkey baster holds using cups of different sizes.

Developmental range: Supporting children at different levels

Earlier ⟶

Children may

- Pour water from one cup into another (to explore pouring).
- Partially fill the cup or baster (not attempt to fill it fully) and/or fill it to a different level each time.
- Squirt water into multiple cups.
- Not count the number of basters full of water squirted into the cup.
- Rote count rather than count each squirt of the baster.
- Say how much water the cup holds in nonnumerical terms (e.g., *It holds a bunch; Only a little in this one*).
- Not compare or order the sizes of cups.

Adults can

- Ask children if the baster or cup can hold more water (e.g., *Is the cup (baster) full or do you think it can hold more water?*).
- Count each time the child fills or empties the baster.
- Prompt children after they add another baster full of water (e.g., *How many basters have you added so far? Is the cup full or is there room to add more?*).
- Use comparative terms related to volume, such as *less* and *least; greater* and *greatest*. Note whether a cup holds the least or greatest amount (volume) of water.
- Encourage children to order and compare cups (e.g., *Can you help me find a cup that holds more water than this one? I'm looking for the cup that holds the least amount of water*).

Middle ⟶

Children may

- (Attempt to) fill the baster before each squirt; repeat same procedure each time.
- Fill cup(s) to measure how much each one holds.
- Count basters but not necessarily correctly (may lose track, skip or repeat a number, count numbers out of order).
- Represent fractional amounts of water used to fill basters by rounding off to whole numbers (e.g., call 2½ basters either "2" or "3" basters).
- Compare and order cup sizes visually but not numerically (may order them from smallest to biggest, or vice versa, but not compare how many basters of water each size holds) (e.g., *The big cup holds more water than the little cup; This is an in-between cup*).

Adults can

- Model strategies to keep track of counting (e.g., have one person fill and squirt while another counts; use tally marks or objects).
- Emphasize that the last number counted tells how many basters full of water the cup holds (e.g., *One, two, three. This cup holds three basters of water*).
- Comment on nonwhole numbers (e.g., *This cup holds between two and three basters of water*).
- Encourage children to compare cup sizes (volume) numerically (e.g., *The biggest cup holds five cups. How many do you think the smallest one will hold?*).
- Model making tally marks for each number counted; make mark immediately after squirting so as not to lose track.

Later ⟶

Children may

- Correctly count the number of basters filled with water; state the last number counted as the total number.
- Ask how to count nonwhole numbers (e.g., *Three whole basters and just some of the last one. How many is that?*).
- Compare and order cup sizes based on the number of basters full of water they hold (e.g., *seven and five and two basters. That's the biggest to the littlest*).
- Predict whether a cup will hold more or less water than another cup based on their relative sizes.
- Use smaller cups to measure volume of larger cups (e.g., *Four small is the same amount of water as one big*).

Adults can

- Put cups in the wrong order. See if children correct the mistake; or say, *Something doesn't look right. Can you help me fix it?*
- Ask children to predict how many more (or fewer) basters of water a bigger (or smaller) cup will hold. Encourage children to verify their guesses.
- Introduce terms related to volume (e.g., *We call the amount a container holds the* volume; *It's still halfway empty*).
- Model using columns or different pieces of paper to tally the volume for each cup size.
- Encourage children to measure volume using different units (e.g., cups, basters) and compare them.

20 How Tall Is My Teacher?

Children use different sizes of shoes to estimate, measure, record, and compare measurements of the teacher's height.

Time of day: Small-Group Time

Content area: Mathematics

Materials

Materials for each child and teacher:

- 1 adult-sized dress-up shoe
- 1 child-sized shoe (children may enjoy trading shoes)
- Butcher paper with a full body outline of the teacher [Note: If your children can work together, make one outline for every two children]

Shared materials:

- Markers/crayons for recording measurements

Backup materials:

- Conventional tools (e.g., rulers, yardsticks) or unconventional objects (e.g., a unit block, plastic banana, storybook, pillow) that can be used for measurement

Beginning

- Trace copies of your body outline prior to class, and tape one copy to the wall. Ask the children *How tall do you think I am?* Record the estimates inside the outline. If children make unit-based estimates, note the unit of measurement (e.g., one hundred feet, a thousand inches).
- Tell them *I want to know how many shoes tall I am. Can you help me measure?* Use your shoe and measure your outline with the children's help. Model and talk about measurement techniques. Begin at the bottom of the outline and place your shoe where the previous shoe unit ended. Ask the children for their measurement suggestions (e.g., *Where should I put the shoe now? How can we keep count of how many we already measured?*).

- Record the group measurement on the butcher paper outline and say *We measured that I am ___ shoe units tall.*
- Give each child (or pair of children) an outline of your body and an adult-sized dress-up shoe. Ask children to also use one of their own shoes. Encourage them to measure how tall you are using the different-sized shoes and the outline of your body. Say something like *I wonder how many shoes tall I'll be. Let's see what you find out.*
  [Note: Some children may want to work in groups of three or more, others may want to work alone. Accept their preferences as long as each has easy access to an outline.]

Middle

- Encourage children to measure how tall you are in different shoe units and to record (or have you record) the number on the outline.
- Encourage the children to share and discuss with you and their peers the different measurements of your height. Guide the discussion toward the idea of different units (different lengths or shoe sizes) affecting the result.

End

- Ask the children for suggestions on where to store the body outlines in case they want to do more measuring at work/choice time.
- Ask the children to count the distance in their own shoe units as they move to the next activity. Demonstrate putting the heel up against the toe of the previous step. Ask if they think it will take them more or fewer steps than you to get there. Help them count to verify their estimates.

Ideas for follow-up

- Ask families to bring in old shoes of different sizes (children's and adult's). Keep them in a container along with both conventional and unconventional measuring tools.
- Provide butcher block paper for children to trace and measure other objects and people in the classroom and outside. Encourage children to collaborate (e.g., to trace one another; to have one child move the measuring tool while the other counts or makes tally marks).
- Do heel-toe walking and counting at large-group time.

Adaptations for children with special needs

- For children with visual limitations, mark the top and bottom of the outline (head and feet) by taping small blocks or other objects the child can easily feel. Help the child walk, crawl, or stretch his or her hands along the length of the outline to get a physical sense of the distance from top to bottom.
- For children who cannot write or see numerals and tally marks, provide small objects (e.g., counting bears, toothpicks) the child can feel and count.

Developmental range: Supporting children at different levels

Earlier ⟶

Children may
- Line up shoes next to one another.
- Make nonnumerical, nonunit-based estimates of teacher's height (e.g., *Really, really, tall*).
- Make exaggerated estimates (e.g., *100 big shoes*).
- Begin measuring in the middle of the teacher's outline rather than from the bottom (or top).
- Measure teacher's body width as opposed to height.
- Miscount the number of shoe units they have measured.
- Not connect different units of measurement (e.g., dress-up shoe, child's shoe) to differences in measurements of the teacher's height.

Adults can
- Comment on relative shoe sizes; say which is longer or shorter.
- Encourage relative estimates of height (e.g., *How many of you would it take to make one of me?*).
- Provide unit-based measurement benchmarks in the classroom (e.g., *The book cabinet is about two feet tall*).
- Explicitly connect the terms *height* and *width* to these dimensions on the outline.
- Demonstrate marking where one shoe unit ends and the next one begins.
- Count as you measure, emphasizing one-to-one correspondence; repeat the last number counted as the total number of units.

Middle ⟶

Children may
- Make nonnumerical, relative estimates (e.g. *You're as tall as my dad; You're taller than my mom*).
- Make exaggerated unit-based estimates (e.g., *100 feet*).
- Make estimates mixing different units of measurement (e.g., *That weighs six pounds, three miles*).
- Be aware of but unable to explain why the teacher's height is different when measured with different-sized shoes.
- Measure without marking, or by inaccurately marking, where the previous unit ended.
- Count the number of units aloud, possibly misremembering.

Adults can
- Give children a unit-based framework for estimates (e.g., *You are about 3½ feet tall. How tall do you think I am?*).
- Re-model the measuring process; focus on continuing the measurement where the previous unit ended.
- Ask children, *How can you keep track of how many shoe units you have measured?* Suggest keeping tally marks of the number of units.
- Encourage children to compare the relative size of their shoe with other (teacher or dress-up) shoes.

Later ⟶

Children may
- Make reasonable numerical estimates of the teacher's height using appropriate units (e.g., *five feet; two yards*).
- Begin measuring at the bottom (or top) of the outline and attempt to make the end of one shoe continuous with the next shoe.
- Utilize tallies to keep track of each additional shoe unit they measure.
- Predict different measurement results based on differences in shoe sizes.

Adults can
- Encourage children to estimate the heights (in shoe units) of other people they know at home and in school.
- Encourage children to measure the teacher's outline again using other unconventional and conventional measuring tools.
- Emphasize the measurement process is the same regardless of the tool or unit used (e.g., shoes and rulers).
- Compare shoe sizes (adult and child) and ruler size. Discuss how shoe-unit sizes are shorter or longer than ruler units and how that difference affects measurement results.

21 Play Dough Snowmen

Children describe, record, tally, and compare the type and number of shapes they use to create play dough snowmen.

Time of day: Small-Group Time **Content Area:** Mathematics

Materials

Materials for each child and teacher:

- Play dough (make sure the dough is "stiff" enough to cut)
- Shape cookie cutters (e.g., triangle, rectangle, circle); may substitute plastic knives for cookie cutters

Shared materials:

- Chart paper with three columns, one for each shape (e.g., triangle, rectangle, circle); label each column with a picture of the shape
- Small paper triangles, rectangles, and circles (to place on the chart paper)

Backup materials:

- Items children can use to decorate the snowmen (e.g., small bits of construction paper, yarn, buttons, shells, twigs)

Beginning

- Talk to the children about their previous experiences making snowmen.
- Say *Sometimes people make snowmen with circles. But today we're going to make them with other shapes too.* With the children, point to and name the cookie-cutter shapes, or cut out shapes from the dough with plastic knives and name them.
- Model cutting out two to three play dough shapes (e.g., two rectangles, or two circles and a triangle) and putting them together to form a snowman. (It's easier if snowmen lie flat on the table, but accept that some children may try to make theirs stand upright.)
- Provide children with shape cookie cutters (or plastic knives) and play dough, and encourage them to make their own play dough snowmen.

Say *Let's see how many of these shapes we'll use to make our snowmen.*

Middle

- Provide shape names and encourage children to name and describe the shapes they use.
- Use *none, some,* and *all* to comment on the shapes children do (or do not) use. Refer to the number of each type of shape. For example, you might say, *Jason and Kimmy used some rectangles and some circles, but no triangles in their snowmen; Your snowman has one square and two circles.*
- After each child shares his or her snowman with the group, say *Let's see how many of each kind of shape we used all together.* Ask children to pick out the corresponding type and number of paper shapes and put them in the appropriate column on the chart paper. Children may count the total first and then pick out that number of shapes. Or, to help children with one-to-one correspondence, encourage them to pick out a shape as they count off each number. (Alternatively, you or the children could draw each shape in the appropriate column.) Encourage children to name and count the shapes as they are added to the chart.
- Align the shapes going down each column. Looking at the chart, talk about which shapes were used the most and the least in making the snowmen. Encourage children to compare the length of each line of shapes, as well as to count them.

End

- Together with the children, put the cookie cutters, play dough, and any unused paper shapes away. Post the shape chart on the wall.

- Ask the children to move "like snowmen" on their way to the next activity. As they move, ask what shape(s) they represent.

Ideas for follow-up

- Make snowmen with additional shapes (e.g., diamonds, trapezoids, hexagons).
- Decorate play dough or paper snowmen, and chart differences in the attributes of the decorations the children use, such as types of materials (e.g., buttons, yarn, shells); snowman's facial and head features (e.g., eyes, nose, hair); clothing (e.g., hats, belts, scarves); and so on. Chart them with pieces of the same materials or with other small objects or tally marks.

Adaptations for children with special needs

- Children can work on their wheelchair trays instead of at the table.
- For children who have trouble manipulating the materials, help them cut out and assemble their shapes. Follow their directions. Encourage their peers to help them.
- Encourage children with visual disabilities to feel around the edges of the cookie cutters and shapes and to describe what they are feeling. With their permission, guide their hands to feel and count the type and number of each shape. State the names of the shapes other children put on the chart, and keep a running verbal tally.

In this activity, children use cookie cutters and plastic knives to make different shapes with play dough.

Developmental range: Supporting children at different levels

Earlier ⟶   **Middle** ⟶   **Later** ⟶

Earlier

Children may

- Describe their snowman without reference to shapes (e.g., focus on color or decorations, state whether it is tall or short).
- Name but not quantify shapes (e.g., *I used circles and rectangles*); may miscount some shapes.
- Place the wrong shape(s) or number of shapes on the chart paper (e.g., use a circle and two triangles, but put three circles on the chart paper).

Adults can

- Talk about snowmen using shape names; name and comment on the shapes children are using.
- Comment on children's snowmen in numerical terms (e.g., *You used one circle and two triangles*).
- Point to each shape on children's snowmen and help them find a corresponding paper shape to put on the chart. Label each shape as it is placed on the chart.
- Model charting snowman's shapes (e.g., *My snowman has two circles and one triangle, so I'm putting two circles and one triangle on our chart*).
- Point out the shortest and longest column and say those shapes that were used the most/least.

Middle

Children may

- Describe their snowman in terms of shape; may (or may not) label shapes correctly.
- Describe their snowman in numerical terms; may (or may not) use numbers correctly.
- Use the terms *some, none,* and *all* to describe the shapes they do (or do not) use.
- Place the correct shapes and number of shapes on the chart paper.
- Interpret the chart in nonnumerical terms (e.g., *We used lots of circles*).

Adults can

- Encourage children to describe their snowman in shape and numerical terms.
- Point at shapes in the snowmen and on the chart, and ask children to describe and compare their attributes.
- Ask children to compare shapes and numbers in their snowman with those of other children (e.g., *You used all circles. Do you see any others like yours? Can you find some that are different? How?*).
- Ask children to name the shapes that were used by *all, some,* or *none* of the children in the group.
- Ask children which shapes were used more or less often. Ask, *How can you tell?* Help them count the number of shapes in each column.

Later

Children may

- Describe their snowman correctly in terms of shape and number (e.g., *I used one green circle and two red triangles*).
- Describe the attributes of the shapes, e.g., *Mine has two triangles; 1...2...3...4...5...6 points!*
- Use the terms *some, none,* and *all* to describe the totality of particular shapes on the chart (e.g., *All the snowmen had circles but only some had rectangles and triangles*).
- Interpret the chart in numerical terms (e.g., *There's six circles, five triangles, and two rectangles. We used circles the most*).

Adults can

- Ask children about the similarities and differences in the attributes of the shapes.
- Ask children which shape is being used by the most/fewest children. Ask how they know. Encourage them to answer in numerical terms. If necessary, help them count.
- Ask children to predict which column will be longest/shortest (have the most/fewest of each paper shape) on the chart. Record and verify their predictions when the chart is completed.
- Looking at the chart, ask which shape was used the most, next most, and so on, down to the least. Ask how they can check their answers.

22 Rhythm Stick Patterns

Children use a rhythm stick to tap out different patterns on blocks and other objects.

Time of day: Small-Group Time   **Content area:** Mathematics

Materials

Materials for each child and teacher:

- 1 rhythm stick and 2 blocks (wood, plastic, or foam), each a different color

Shared materials:

- None

Backup materials:

- Blocks in different colors and sizes

Beginning

- Hold a rhythm stick and set two blocks on the table in front of you. Tap an *ABABAB* pattern three times and say *red, blue; red, blue; red, blue.* (Always repeat a pattern at least three times.)
- Say *That was a pattern because I patted red, blue; red, blue; red, blue over and over. I can tap a different pattern.* Demonstrate, and then say *red, red, blue; red, red, blue; red, red, blue.*
- Give each child a rhythm stick and two blocks, each a different color, and say *I wonder what patterns you can tap with your sticks.*

Middle

- Encourage children to say their patterns aloud.
- Encourage children to watch and match the patterns other children create.
- Tap and say different patterns with your blocks: *red, red, blue, blue; red, red, blue, blue; red, red, blue, blue.*
- Create tapping patterns based on features other than color, such as sound (loud and soft; single and double taps); size of blocks (large and small); tapping target (top and bottom of block; block and tabletop), and so on.

End

- Together with the children, sort the blocks by color (and/or size) and put them away. Put away the rhythm sticks.
- Ask children to pretend to be sticks and to "tap" their way to the next activity.

Ideas for follow-up

- Tap patterns during transitions to help children settle down and begin the next activity (e.g., loud, loud, soft; loud, loud, soft; loud, loud, soft).
- Ask children to suggest other materials they might use to create tapping patterns (e.g., tapping a small toy on a table and chair in an alternating rhythm).
- Write patterns with markers in corresponding colors on a dry-erase board for children to copy.
- At large-group time, pat different body parts in a pattern (e.g., head, shoulders; head, shoulders; head, shoulders); ask for suggestions from children and encourage them to show/tell their pattern for others to copy.

Adaptations for children with special needs

- For children with visual limitations, provide two objects they can tap to make different sounds (e.g., wooden and plastic blocks; bell and block).
- For children with auditory limitations, add visual elements to emphasize the patterns (e.g., clap over your head when the blue block is tapped; clap in front of your body when the red block is tapped).

- Encourage children who are not able to grasp rhythm sticks to tap objects with open hands, touch them with their toes, and so on.

- For children who are bothered by the sound, provide foam blocks or other non-noisy objects to tap. They may want to do the activity at a distance from the other children if the tapping noises upset them.

Developmental range: Supporting children at different levels

Earlier ⟶

Children may
- Name the colors of their blocks (e.g., *I got blue and yellow*).
- Tap blocks in random fashion.
- Tap two blocks once in alternation but not continue the pattern.
- Copy an *ABABAB* pattern initiated by the teacher or another child.

Adults can
- Copy the sequences a child makes, whether random or patterned.
- Tap a pattern and encourage children to copy it.
- Tap a child's pattern and say it aloud (e.g., *You tapped red, green; red, green; red, green*).

Middle ⟶

Children may
- Tap an *ABABAB* pattern with their blocks.
- Describe their pattern while tapping (e.g., *I tapped yellow, green, yellow, green*).
- Copy an *AABBAABBAABB* or *AABAABAAB* pattern.

Adults can
- Talk about tapping the blocks over and over again (i.e., the idea that patterns repeat).
- Introduce an *AABBAAB-BAABB* pattern (e.g., *Here's a new pattern: Red, red, blue, blue; red, red, blue, blue; red, red, blue, blue*).
- Encourage children to create an *AABBAABBAABB* pattern.

Later ⟶

Children may
- Identify a tapping sequence as a pattern (e.g., *It's a pattern 'cause it goes over and over*).
- Extend someone else's pattern (say where to tap next).
- Create an *AABBAABBAABB* or *AABAABAAB* pattern.
- Create a pattern using a feature other than color (e.g., *block, tabletop; block, tabletop; block, tabletop*).

Adults can
- Ask children to suggest a pattern and copy it (e.g., *Tell me a pattern to tap with my blocks*).
- Ask children how to copy their pattern (e.g., *How can I tap a pattern like yours with my blocks?*).
- Stop tapping and ask children, *What color block do I tap next?*
- Create sequences (patterned or random) and ask children whether they are patterns.
- Deliberately make an error and see if the children catch and correct it.
- Tap patterns that depend on other features, such as sound (e.g., *loud, soft; loud, soft; loud, soft*).

23 Shape Caterpillars

Children arrange cut-out shapes in a pattern to make a "caterpillar."

Time of day: Small-Group Time   **Content Area:** Mathematics

Materials

Materials for each child and teacher:
- Small circles and rectangles, 5–10 of each, cut out of construction paper (use one color, the same for both shapes)
- 1 sheet of blank paper

Shared materials:
- None

Backup materials:
- Glue stick

Beginning
- Place a circle on a blank piece of paper before you.
- Begin a story by saying *Once upon a time, there was a very small caterpillar. He was made of just one circle.*
- Put a rectangle next to the circle and say *But then it ate a rectangle and grew longer!*
- Continue the story by adding another circle and a rectangle, then another circle and rectangle (three repeats in all). Call children's attention to the pattern by saying *It looks as if the caterpillar is eating a pattern: rectangle, circle; rectangle, circle; rectangle, circle. As the caterpillar eats the pattern, it gets longer and longer!*

Middle
- Give each child a set of circles and rectangles and a piece of paper.
- Say something like *Here are some circles and rectangles for you to use. I wonder what your caterpillars will look like.*

- As the children work, name and talk to them about the shape(s) they are using. Point to and recite the order of their shapes. Comment on whether they are arranging the shapes in a pattern. Copy the patterns children make. Ask them to tell you the order or pattern of their shapes so you can make a caterpillar like theirs. Start a pattern and ask children to help you continue (extend) it or to fill in a missing shape.
- After the children have had time to manipulate and arrange some of their shapes, distribute the glue.

End
- After children have cleaned up their materials, ask them to move "like caterpillars" to the next activity.

Ideas for follow-up
- Add shapes (cut from paper, felt, foam, etc.) to the art area.
- Use a single shape but in two colors to pattern a "color caterpillar."
- Give children three shapes (circle, rectangle, triangle) of a single color to create patterns.

Adaptations for children with special needs
- For children with visual and/or manipulative limitations, use shape blocks (e.g., wood or plastic) they can feel and/or handle more easily than paper cutouts.

Developmental range: Supporting children at different levels

Earlier ⟶

Children may
- Place shapes all over their paper.
- Line up the shapes in random order.
- Describe how they lined up their shapes (e.g., *Mine goes circle, circle, circle, rectangle, circle, rectangle;* or *Mine's all the same*).

Adults can
- Describe how the child has arranged shapes (e.g., *You covered your whole paper with circles and triangles*).
- Line up shapes (e.g., *I'm going to make my caterpillar grow. Gulp, it ate a circle. Gulp, it ate a rectangle*).

Middle ⟶

Children may
- Copy the teacher's or another child's simple *ABABAB* pattern.
- Create a simple *ABABAB* pattern.
- Describe a pattern as repeating (e.g., *You have to make the same things over and over*).

Adults can
- Encourage children to describe how they have arranged the shapes.
- Create a simple *ABABAB* pattern and encourage the child to copy it (e.g., *My caterpillar is lonely. I wonder if you could make one that looks the same as mine*).
- Use the words *pattern* or *over and over again* (e.g., *My caterpillar's pattern is circle, rectangle; circle, rectangle; circle, rectangle — over and over again*).
- Place a circle and a rectangle on the child's paper, then encourage the child to repeat the process to create a pattern.

Later ⟶

Children may
- Extend the teacher's or another child's simple *ABABAB* pattern.
- Spot a mistake in their own or someone else's simple pattern and correct it.
- Recognize a complex repeating sequence (e.g., *AABB-AABBAABB; AABAABAAB*) as a pattern.
- Create a complex pattern (e.g., *AABBAABBAABB; AABAABAAB*).

Adults can
- Change the orientation of a pattern (e.g., from vertical to horizontal), and ask children if the sequence still makes a pattern.
- Create a pattern and ask the child to extend it (e.g., *My caterpillar wants more to eat. Would you like to feed it so its pattern grows?*).
- Make a mistake or leave a blank in a pattern, and ask the child to correct it or fill it in (e.g., *My caterpillar ate two circles in a row. Can you help fix its pattern?*).
- Create a complex sequence (e.g., *AABAABAAB; AABB-AABBAABB*), and ask children if it makes a pattern.
- Encourage the child to make a complex pattern (e.g., *AABBAABBAABB* or *AAB-AABAAB*).

Adults can describe and copy children's patterns, pointing to the shapes children use and saying their names in order.

24 Shape Hopscotch

Children pick a shape from a bag, then jump to the square with a matching shape on a hopscotch board.

Time of day: Small-Group Time

Content Area: Mathematics

Materials

Materials for each child and teacher:

- 6-square hopscotch board drawn on large sheets of butcher paper or made of masking tape on the floor (it can also be chalked on the ground if small-group time takes place outside); the board should be one column (or row), six squares long with boxes large enough for children to jump into easily

- 3 large shape cards: (circle, triangle, and rectangle)
- Small paper cutouts of each of the three shapes — circles, triangles, and rectangles (including squares) in different sizes (e.g., 5 large, 5 medium, and 5 small circles; 5 large, 5 medium, and 5 small triangles)
- Container filled with the small cutouts

Shared materials:

- Chart with three columns, each labeled at the top with a drawing or cutout of one of the shapes
- Tape

Backup materials:

- Extra small, medium, and large shapes

Beginning

- Tell the children you are going to play shape hopscotch. Model the game:
  — Put a large shape card in each of three hopscotch squares (e.g., the triangle in the first square, the rectangle in the fourth square, and the circle in the sixth square).
  — Pick a shape out of the container. Name the shape and describe its attributes (e.g., *I picked a triangle. It has three sides and three points*).
  — Hop (or jump) to the square with the matching shape.
  — Walk to the chart and tape or place the shape you picked in the appropriate column.
- Move the large shapes to different squares on the hopscotch board and repeat.
- Give each child a set of materials and say *Now you can play shape hopscotch with your own hopscotch boards and shapes.*

Middle

- Support children as they pick shapes from their containers and put their large shapes on their hopscotch board.
- Encourage children to describe the attributes of the shapes they pick. Comment that regardless of the size, it is still the same shape.
- Encourage children to move the large shapes to different squares on the board after each turn.
- After each turn, ask the child to tape the shape they picked from the container onto the appropriate column of the chart. (Some children may want to continue playing the game without using the chart.)

End

- Looking at the chart, point out the different-sized shapes in each column and emphasize again that they are still all the same shape, regardless of size. Review the attributes of each shape.
- With the children, count how many of each shape they chose during the game. Comment on which shape was chosen most or least often,

whether shapes were chosen the same number of times, and so on.

- With the children, sort the leftover shapes and decide where to store them so that children can continue to use them.
- Encourage the children to hop or jump to the next activity.

Ideas for follow-up

- Play shape hopscotch with other shapes (e.g., diamonds, trapezoids, hexagons).
- Give children paper, drawing materials, and scissors to draw, cut out, and sort the types of shapes used in the hopscotch game.
- Play numeral hopscotch (children pick numerals instead of shapes out of a bag); begin with numerals 1–5 and later in the year use numerals 0–9.

- Use the hopscotch idea for planning or recall, laying area signs on the hopscotch board. For example, for planning, ask children to jump to the area they would like to play in and then tell you what they are going to do there.

Adaptations for children with special needs

- For children with limited mobility, make a table-sized hopscotch board with squares they can "walk" or "hop" to with their hands. Use doll figures they can "hop" along a smaller board. Children in wheelchairs can wheel their chairs along a board with larger squares that is set out on the floor.
- For children with visual limitations, use shapes they can feel (e.g., wooden, plastic) instead of cards and paper cutouts.

Developmental range: Supporting children at different levels

Earlier ⟶ **Middle** ⟶ **Later** ⟶

Children may

- Use a shape word incorrectly (e.g., identify a rectangle as a triangle).
- Ask for help matching the shape they pick with the large shape on the board (e.g., *Which square do I hop to?*).
- Hop/jump on the hopscotch board without regard to shape.
- Ask which column on the chart to put their shape in.

Adults can

- Name the shape on the square the children hop to; ask where children will hop next.
- Pick a shape and match it to the shape on the hopscotch board (e.g., *I picked a circle. Here's a circle on the board. I'm hopping to it. Do you want to hop to the circle with me?*).
- Encourage children to jump to the square with the shape they picked; name the shape and hop to the corresponding square, saying *I wonder if you can hop to the square with the triangle too.* (Hop/jump alongside child if necessary.)
- Help children place their shapes on the chart (e.g., *You have a rectangle. Which of these* [point to labels on columns] *is the same shape as yours?*).

Children may

- Name the shapes they pick but not describe the attributes.
- Jump/hop to the corresponding shape on the hopscotch board.
- Put the shape they picked in the correct column of the chart.
- Exclude squares as examples of rectangles.
- Be unsure whether different sizes of a shape are the same shape (e.g., hop/jump to the correct hopscotch square when they pick a large circle but be unsure where to jump/hop when they pick a small circle).
- Comment on the different sizes of the shapes.

Adults can

- Describe the attributes of the shapes children pick.
- Count the sides and corners of children's shapes, encouraging them to count the sides and corners of the shapes they are holding.
- Comment/describe how squares and rectangles are the same and different (e.g., *Both have four sides and four points. A square is a kind of rectangle, but all the sides are the same*).
- Discuss the attributes of shapes of the same type but different sizes to help children understand that size differences do not change the shape.

Children may

- Describe one or more attributes of the shapes they pick.
- Understand a shape is a shape regardless of size (e.g., hop/jump to the correct hopscotch square whether they pick a small, medium, or large circle).
- Compare attributes of different shapes (e.g., *Triangles have three points and rectangles have four*).
- Include squares as rectangles.
- Distinguish between shapes (e.g., *I picked circles and triangles; I didn't pick any rectangles*).
- Tally the number of shapes in each column.

Adults can

- Encourage children to provide as many details as they can when describing shapes.
- Encourage children to compare the attributes of different shapes (e.g., *A triangle has three sides and three points. What about a rectangle?*).
- Ask, *How many sides does a circle have?*
- Ask children what attributes a shape does *not* have (e.g., *Can you tell me what this shape has that this one doesn't? Do any of these shapes not have four corners?*).
- Encourage children to tally and compare on the chart the number of each shape picked during the game.

25 Strike Up The Band

Children describe, sort, and compare the sound of musical instruments based on their loudness and softness (and other attributes).

Time of day: Small-Group Time   **Content area:** Mathematics

Materials

Materials for each child and teacher:

- 1 small to medium-sized container with musical instruments and other noisemakers that can be used to make loud and soft sounds (e.g., drums, rhythm sticks, triangles, bells, whistles, pairs of wooden or plastic blocks, sandpaper, rattles, ticking timers)

Shared materials:

- 2 large containers for sorting instruments (the containers should be different, e.g., a basket and a box or different-colored baskets); you can also make "loud" and "quiet" labels (e.g., words, initials, pictures with hands over ears and at sides, photos of loud and quiet items such as a roaring lion and a bumble bee), and let the children decide which label should go on each container

Backup materials:

- Duplicates of instruments if children decide some should go in both the "loud" and "soft/quiet" containers
- Additional large container for "undecided" instruments

Beginning

- Tell the children a story about a "loud" band and a "quiet/soft" band: *Once upon a time there was nest of baby birds. They had to get up early in the morning to hunt for worms. After they ate their worms and played, it was time to take a nap. Mama and Papa bird decided to make a band that played loud music to wake up the baby birds and a band that played quiet music to help them fall asleep. Let's help the Mama and Papa bird make a loud band and a quiet band.*
- Give each child a small container of instruments, and put the two large containers in the middle of the table. Talk briefly with the children about how to label the two containers.

Pick an instrument from your container and play it. Ask the children if it is loud or quiet, and which band it belongs in, then put it in the corresponding container.

- Say *Let's listen to the other instruments in our baskets and decide whether to put each one in the loud band or the quiet band.*

Middle

- Encourage children to try each instrument and decide if it is loud or soft. Engage them in discussing their instruments' attributes. Accept their descriptions and classifications, including their labeling of an instrument as having both attributes (e.g., a triangle can be loud or soft, depending on how hard it is struck). If children are undecided about an instrument, place it in the additional backup container and encourage children to give a name to its sound.

As a follow-up activity, teachers can let children choose an instrument and plan or recall according to whose instrument is loudest, next loudest, and so on (or vice versa).

- Talk about other sound attributes and similarities and differences in how instruments are played (e.g., *That's rumbly, like thunder; You need two hands to play this one but only one hand for this one; The rattle makes noise by shaking and the blocks by banging*).
- Stop periodically to count the instruments in each container. Compare which has more or fewer and by how many. Ask children to predict how many of each instrument will be in each band when they are finished with listening and sorting. Record their predictions and refer back to them at the end of the activity.

End

- Count and compare the number of instruments in each band; review which band has more or fewer instruments and by how many. Compare the actual number in each band to the predicted/estimated numbers.
- Tell the children it's time to wake the baby birds one last time. Let them choose instruments from the "loud" container and play a wakeup song. Then say it's time for the activity to end and for the baby birds to go to sleep; ask them to choose instruments from the "quiet" container and play a "go-to-sleep" song. If you have the equipment, record the children's songs and play them back.
- Remind the children where the instruments and noisemakers are stored should they want to use them at work/choice time.
- Ask the children to each pick one instrument or noisemaker. Say something like *Whoever has a loud instrument, put it in the loud container and* stomp *to* [the next activity]. *Now, whoever has a quiet instrument, put it in the quiet container and* tiptoe *to* [the next activity].

Ideas for follow-up

- At planning time, let children choose an instrument from a container and plan according to who has the loudest, next loudest, and so on. At recall, repeat the process but go in order according to quietness (softness).
- At large-group time, distribute instruments. Let the children form a band, deciding on the attribute(s) they want to include. Let children take turns choosing an attribute (e.g., instruments that can be played with one hand, shaking instruments, instruments with low/high pitch).
- Add new instruments and noisemakers to the classroom. Encourage parents to contribute similar items from home. As you add each new item, encourage children to describe its characteristics and compare it to existing items in the collection.
- At planning time, record children's plans. At recall time, replay the recording and ask children to guess who is speaking. Ask the speaker to share what he or she did at work time.

Adaptations for children with special needs

- Children who cannot grasp or manipulate instruments may be able to hit a drum or bang on a keyboard that is secured on the table. They can also listen as the teacher and/or other children play instruments.
- Children with auditory limitations that make it difficult to discriminate loudness may be able to feel the difference in vibrations caused by various noisemakers, hear extremes in pitch (choose instruments and noisemakers pitched very low and very high), or hear and/or feel vibrations of continuous versus interrupted sounds.

Developmental range: Supporting children at different levels

Earlier →

Children may

- Play with the instruments but not sort or label them as *loud* or *quiet*.
- Not understand the meaning of (or the difference between) the words *loud* and *quiet*.
- Say all the instruments are loud (or all the instruments are quiet).
- Sort instruments but make errors in sorting (e.g., say an instrument is *loud* but put it in the container labeled "quiet" or vice versa).
- Sort instruments but not be able to state the reason (e.g., *It just goes there*).
- Compare instruments nonnumerically (e.g., *The loud band has more; There are only a few in the soft basket but lots in the loud box*).

Adults can

- Demonstrate a loud versus quiet sound.
- Encourage children to make loud and quiet sounds with two instruments (e.g., *Can you make a loud noise with this? Pick another and let's see if you can make a quiet noise with it*).
- Ask children to compare instruments and to say how the sounds are the same or different.
- Ask children to sort instruments onto their corresponding containers. Confirm the child's choice (e.g., *Is that the basket you want to put the blocks in?*). Accept the response even if it seems to contradict the child's choice.
- Encourage children to count the instruments in each container. Model one-to-one correspondence and other counting strategies.

Middle →

Children may

- Sort instruments correctly into loud and quiet containers.
- Not recognize or acknowledge that an instrument may be both loud and quiet, depending on how it is played.
- Sort instruments and state the reason (e.g., *When you shake the rattle, it's loud, but when you shake the beanbag, it just makes a little whooshy sound*).
- Describe (but not compare) other attributes of the instruments (e.g., *It* [the metronome] *goes* click, click, click *like a clock; The triangle has two shapes, a triangle and a stick*).
- Count but not compare the instruments in each band.

Adults can

- Encourage children to describe the reasons for their sorting. Ask them to compare two instruments (e.g., *What makes you say this one is loud but that one is quiet? What's the same about the two you say are quiet? How are these two sounds different?*).
- Intentionally put an instrument in the wrong container and see if children spot the mistake. If not, play the instrument the same way the child did (e.g., as loud or quiet) and ask, *Did I put this in the right container?*
- Encourage children to observe and describe other attributes of the instruments.
- Encourage children to state which container has more/ fewer instruments.

Later →

Children may

- Explain that an instrument can be either loud or quiet (e.g., *If I bang the blocks together, it's really loud, but if I just tap them they go in the quiet band*).
- Describe and compare other attributes of the instruments (e.g., *The sticks you hold in your hands, but the xylophone goes on the table; This is made of wood and this one is metal*).
- Count and compare the instruments in each band (e.g., *There's four loud and only two soft, so we got two more loud so far*).
- Predict/estimate the total number of instruments there will be in each band, (e.g., *We're gonna have three extra loud ones because the babies don't want to go to sleep*).

Adults can

- Encourage children to order three or more instruments (e.g., *Which is the loudest? next loudest? quietest?*).
- Ask children how to sort instruments that are both loud and quiet.
- Add new story elements to encourage children to think about other ways to sort instruments (e.g., *The neighbors complained that they didn't like loud noises. How else could Mama and Papa bird make one band for wakeup and another for going to sleep?*).
- Ask children how many more or fewer instruments are in one container compared to another. Ask how many need to be added or subtracted to make them the same.
- Ask if children's predictions were correct or incorrect and by how many.

IV. Science and Technology

A hundred or more years ago, science primarily involved the study and classification of nature. As chemistry and physics took their place alongside biology, science became increasingly concerned with how things change when acted upon in different ways. Early science is therefore more than memorizing information about the biological and physical world. Curriculum developers and researchers Rochel Gelman and Kimberly Brenneman point out that "to do science is to predict, test, measure, count, record, date one's work, collaborate and communicate" (2004, p. 156). In other words, science is as much about the investigative process as it is about knowing facts and formulas. And science also uses math, literacy, and social skills.

Early science learning has many parallels to early mathematics. Both involve manipulating materials and ideas, observing the properties of objects and events, sorting things according to properties, making predictions about what will happen, and drawing conclusions based on what actually happens. In science, however, children are not only concerned with the quantitative aspects of their world, they also explore its qualitative aspects. As their scientific minds develop, young children are engaged in the following activities:

- **Observing** is paying attention to something to learn about its properties. Preschoolers gather data and make discoveries about the physical world using all their senses. For example, they look at, smell, touch, and taste vegetables in the garden as they simultaneously listen to the humming bees or chirping birds in that environment. Because so much of the world is new to them, young children observe and collect data virtually all the time.
- **Classifying** is sorting or grouping things together, separating and comparing what is the same from what is different based on one or more attributes. This process includes organiz-

ing information, fitting new information into existing categories, or changing categories to fit the new information (for example, recognizing that red beads and blue beads can be further subdivided into small and large beads, that is, beads can be sorted by the attributes of both color and size).
- **Experimenting** is testing an idea to see if it is true (accurate or valid) or trying a solution to see how and if it works. For young children, purposeful exploration is the hallmark of experimentation. They investigate materials and actions to discover their properties and to determine how things change when they are acted upon by people or events. For example, they experiment to see how fast toy cars go when the angle of a ramp changes from shallow to steep.
- **Predicting** is making an "educated guess" (rather than a wild one), based on one's knowledge, however limited that knowledge may be by adult standards. Predicting depends upon being able to hold a picture (mental representation) in mind, an ability that develops gradually in the preschool years. Young children do not always verbalize their predictions, but you can infer them by watching the next step in their experiments or the look of satisfaction (or surprise) when their predictions do (or do not) come true.
- **Drawing conclusions** is describing, reflecting upon, and explaining what one has observed — accurately or not — and then fitting it into one's system of knowledge and understanding. Children construct knowledge in their own way. They form theories and make generalizations based on their experiences. The more varied and in-depth these experiences are, the more data they have upon which to base conclusions.
- **Communicating ideas** is sharing one's questions, observations, predictions, and conclu-

Science is about investigating, not just knowing facts and formulas. Young scientists observe, classify, experiment, predict, draw conclusions, and communicate ideas.

sions with others. Young children, excited by their discoveries, communicate through talking, drawing, writing (using words and symbols), physical demonstrations, and gestures. For example, they may draw a picture and ask the teacher to take dictation describing how they made "popcorn pancakes" by pressing beads into flattened circles of play dough. Recording their ideas in pictures, words, or simple graphs and charts, helps validate the importance of the scientific process.

While being cautious not to overestimate children's abilities (Ginsburg & Golbeck, 2004), educators recognize the appropriateness of introducing science as a distinct content area in the early childhood curriculum. Israeli professors of science and technology education Haim Eshach and Michael Fried (2005) offer six reasons for taking advantage of this window of opportunity in the early years:

- Children naturally enjoy observing and thinking about nature.
- Early exposure to scientific processes and ideas helps to develop positive attitudes toward science.
- Early scientific experiences establish a foundation for later formal education in the sciences.
- Children can understand simple scientific concepts and begin to reason scientifically.
- Using scientifically informed language (e.g., If-then statements) at a young age helps children develop an eventual understanding of more complex scientific concepts (e.g., causality).
- Young children are beginning to reason scientifically, and science experiences help to develop scientific thinking about the world.

Discussions about early science education often raise questions about the use of computers. Educators agree that preschoolers need to be familiar with basic technology to get ready for school. Computers can also play a vital role in learning about other content areas, but only *if* they are used correctly (Hyson, 2003). Rather than emphasizing rote drill-and-practice, software should be age-appropriate, open-ended, and designed to promote discovery. Technology can also increase children's ability to manipulate things; sometimes they can move objects on the screen more easily than they can move actual objects. However, computers should never replace real objects, which provide other sensory feedback and foster motor skills. If your program has computers for children, small-group time is a good way to introduce new software, and appropriate programs can supplement hands-on learning. Also, "contrary to initial fears, computers do not isolate children. Rather they serve as potential catalysts for social interaction" (Clements, 1999, p. 122). When using computers, children solve problems together, talk about what they are doing, help and teach friends, and create rules for cooperation. They often prefer working on the computer with a friend to doing it alone.

In the following small-group activities, young children have the opportunity to act like scientists as they interact with materials and apply their thinking and reasoning abilities to explain what they observe. For more ideas on including science materials throughout the room and creating scientific learning opportunities for young children throughout the day, see *Real Science in Preschool: Here, There, Everywhere* (Neill, 2008).

References

Clements, D. H. (1999). The effective use of computers with young children. In J. V. Copley (Ed.), *Mathematics in the early years*. Reston, VA: National Council of Teachers of Mathematics and National Association for the Education of Young Children, 119–128.

Eshach, H., & Fried, M. N. (2005, September). Should science be taught in early childhood? *Journal of Science Education and Technology, 14*(3), 315–336.

Gelman, R., & Brenneman, K. (2004). Science learning pathways for young children. *Early Childhood Research Quarterly, 19*(1), 150–158.

Ginsburg, H. P., & Golbeck, S. L. (2004). Thoughts on the future of research on mathematics and science learning and education. *Early Childhood Research Quarterly, 19*(1), 1–3.

Hyson, M. (Ed.). (2003). *Preparing early childhood professionals: NAEYC's standards for programs*. Washington, DC: National Association for the Education of Young Children.

Neill, P. (2008). *Real science in preschool: Here, there, and everywhere*. Ypsilanti, MI: HighScope Press.

26 Bubble, Bubble

Children blow bubbles, comparing their attributes and exploring differences in bubbles blown with straws and tin cans.

Time of day: Small-Group Time

Content Area: Science and Technology

Materials

Materials for each child and teacher:

- Tinfoil pie pans containing about an inch of dishwashing liquid and water (check proportions so the solution is neither too watery nor too thick to make bubbles)
- Drinking straws

Shared materials:

- None

Backup materials:

- Tin cans with both ends open (taped if they're sharp)

Beginning

- Say something like *Last week we had bottles of bubbles and bubble wands during outside time. Several of you said that you would like to try the bubbles again, to see if you could make bigger ones or ones with funny shapes.*
- Say *I have some other materials you can use to blow bubbles.* Demonstrate putting a straw into the bubble-making solution in a pie pan, and blow on the straw to make bubbles.
- Give each child a pie pan of dishwashing solution and a straw. Say *Let's see what kinds of bubbles you can make.*

Middle

- Circulate among the children as they experiment with the materials, observing and commenting on what they do. Talk about how they blow their bubbles (e.g., with short/fast or long/slow breaths), what the bubbles look like (e.g., size, shape, colors, shine, how they attach to one another), how the bubbles feel (e.g., soft, wet, squishy), and so on.

- Encourage children to describe and think about what they are doing and seeing, asking questions and making comments such as *Why do you think the bubbles stick together?; Did you blow differently to make the big bubbles and the small bubbles?; I wonder what makes the colors.*
- Keep children focused on the bubbles if they get distracted. For example, if you notice Ella is beginning to get other children wet by splashing in her pie pan, you might suggest she ask Natalia to show her how she blows her bubbles.
- Midway through the activity, introduce the tin cans. Talk to the children about the differences in the bubbles they make with the tin cans compared to those they make with the straws.

End

- Put a large tub or bucket in the middle of the table, and ask children to dump their bubble liquid in the tub. As children are washing their hands, let them know where they will find the materials tomorrow (either in the water table inside or outside, in tubs outside, and so on).
- Ask the children to move "like bubbles" to the next part of the daily routine.

Ideas for follow-up

- Bring the pans of bubble liquid outside, along with a variety of bubble blowers (i.e., blowers that make regular and irregular shapes).
- Encourage children to experiment with the bubbles, for example, to see what happens if they lightly touch the bubble with a wet finger, then touch it with a dry finger.
- Talk about other items that have or produce bubbles, such as shampoo, bubble bath, dishwashing liquid, laundry detergent, the car wash, and so on.

Adaptations for children with special needs

- Encourage children with visual limitations to use their other senses to experience the bubbles (e.g., feel and smell them, listen to hear if they pop).

- For children who have trouble blowing, provide other tools for making bubbles (e.g., egg beaters, bubble wands of different sizes and shapes, pieces of mesh with large holes).

Developmental range: Supporting children at different levels

Earlier →

Children may
- Stir the dishwashing solution with the straw.
- Get excited about the bubbles they are making (e.g., *Bubbles! I'm doing bubbles!*).
- Suck the liquid up into the straw instead of blowing it out the straw.
- Blow many bubbles, pausing to pat and feel the growing mound of bubbles in their pan.
- Pop bubbles at random.

Adults can
- Acknowledge what children are doing (e.g., *You're stirring with the straw and making waves; You blew hard and made your own bubbles*).
- Ask children to blow (on the tip of the adult's finger) like they might if they were blowing out candles on a birthday cake. Share that they have to blow inside the straw the same way.
- Ask children to describe what they are doing and imitate their actions (e.g., *Tell me how to blow bubbles the same way you did; How did you pop your bubbles?*).

Middle →

Children may
- Exclaim about the growing size of their bubble mound (e.g., *Mine's getting hugest!*).
- Count how many bubbles are spilling over the pie pan onto the table (e.g., *I made 1...2...3...4...5, bubbles on the table!*).
- Poke through their bubble mound until they pop all the bubbles.

Adults can
- Use descriptive words to comment on what children are doing (e.g., *You have some large bubbles on this side, Jemal, but tiny little ones on the top*).
- Ask children to suggest a way to blow bubbles that are large (or small, thick, or thin, etc.) and try out the child's ideas.
- Use descriptive words to encourage children to describe what they notice (e.g., *Mine feels soft like the top of my kitten's head*).

Later →

Children may
- Begin to notice cause and effect (e.g., *If you blow really hard, you get millions of tiny bubbles*).
- Notice differences in their bubbles (e.g., *The ones I made with the straw are strongest, not the ones with the can — they pop easy*).
- Notice the colors in the bubbles (e.g., *This one looks like a rainbow*).

Adults can
- Ask children to predict what will happen if they blow really hard, really slow.
- Ask children to talk about differences in the bubbles made with the can and the straw. Accept their explanation(s) about why those differences exist. Comment and encourage them to elaborate on their ideas (e.g., *So are you saying these are bigger because the hole is bigger?; You think the colors are from the metal in the can?*).
- Add new vocabulary (e.g., *transparent, translucent, iridescent*) when commenting on bubbles.

27 Cars and Ramps

Children construct ramps for small cars/objects as they explore concepts of velocity and weight.

Time of day: Small-Group Time

Content Area: Science and Technology

Materials

Materials for each child and teacher:

- 2–3 small (Matchbox size) cars
- Long cardboard tubes, large enough in diameter for the cars/balls (see *Backup Materials*, below) to pass through easily; or the ingredients for building a ramp such as 3–5 rectangular unit blocks and some long planks or flexible car tracks
- Basket or similar container for materials

Shared materials:

- Materials for propping one end of the ramp at different heights (e.g., blocks, books, pillows)

Backup materials:

- Round objects such as small balls of different sizes and weights (e.g., ping-pong, solid, and hollow rubber balls; marbles).
- Small objects of other shapes and sizes (e.g., dice, small pieces of crumpled tinfoil).

Beginning

- Say something like *Yesterday in the block area, some trucks went down the ramp fast and far and others went slow or stopped. I wonder why.* Listen to and support the children's explanations.
- Give each child a basket and say *In your baskets you will find some materials to help us figure out why some of the trucks went faster and farther than others. Let's go over to the rug* [or another open area in the room] *so we have plenty of space to spread out.* Together with the children, carry the baskets and props to an open area of the room.

Middle

- Move around the rug and talk to children about what they are doing. Encourage them to describe what they're doing and observing.
- Listen for words that indicate children's developing recognition of the relationship between the grade of the ramp and the speed of the objects traveling on it (e.g., *When I tip this end up, the car goes down real fast*). Accept and repeat the children's words and add new vocabulary words (e.g., *slope, height, angle, fast(er), slow(er), zoom, speed, velocity*).

End

- Together with the children, dismantle the ramps. Remind children where the materials are stored should they want to use them at work time.
- Suggest the children drive a pretend car to the next activity. Ask them if they will move like cars on a hill or cars on a flat road.

Ideas for follow-up

- Add additional road and ramp-building materials (e.g., trays, cutting boards, flattened cartons) to the classroom.
- Encourage children to experiment with rolling objects down naturally-inclined surfaces and/or those they create in the outdoor area (e.g., hills, sand mounds).
- Put books, magazines, and catalogs about racing and race cars in the reading and writing area.
- Provide simple measuring tools, conventional and unconventional (e.g., yardstick, tape, string), and encourage children to compare the heights of the ramps they construct at other small-group times.

Adaptations for children with special needs

- Children with upper-body mobility in a wheel-chair can do the activity at a table, or use their wheelchair table, with all the same materials.

- Children with severe physical impairments can lie on the floor and use shorter cardboard tubes and rubber balls that do not require them to move from one end of the ramp to the other.

In this activity, children investigate the relationship between the slope of the incline and how fast and far their toy cars travel.

Developmental range: Supporting children at different levels

Earlier ⟶ **Middle** ⟶ **Later** ⟶

Children may

- Drive the car around the floor.
- Hit a ball with a long tube and say, *I play golf.*
- Yell *Rrrr, zoooom,* while making a racecar go back and forth on the board.
- Collect several ping-pong balls and put them in a tube, then hold each end, shake it back and forth and say, *Listen.*

Children may

- Say to another child, *Let's have a race* as they place their tracks side by side.
- Comment on what they see happening, comparing different effects (e.g., *The dice make a different sound in the tube than the marbles, and you can't hear the foil*).
- Say, *The cars work best on the tracks — they don't like the tubes.*

Children may

- Comment, *When you add more blocks, the road gets higher and the cars go faster.*
- Say, *Maybe if we pile blocks on both sides and put a long plank across, we can make a bridge.*
- Make a tall pile of blocks at one end of the ramp and say, *When it's high like this, the cars goes all the way to the other side of the block area!*

Adults can

- Join the children on their level and use an "I" statement to make sure no one gets hit (e.g., *I'm hitting gently into an open space so that my ball doesn't hit anyone*).
- Play with materials in parallel with children, exploring how the vehicles move on the ramp.
- Acknowledge how children are using the materials (e.g., *I see you made a shaker from your tube and then put something inside it to make noise. I wonder what it is*).

Adults can

- Join children on the floor as they are racing their cars. Talk about how fast their cars are going (e.g., *Yes, I see your race car is going fast. I wonder what you could do to make it go faster*).
- Talk to the children about their discoveries (e.g., *Did you try the dice and marbles and foil in the tube all at once or one at a time? I wonder what you found out*).
- Encourage children to explain what they observe; ask, *What makes you think that the cars don't like the tubes?*

Adults can

- Pose challenges and "what if" questions (e.g., *I wonder how high it would have to get before the cars stopped racing and just fell off*).
- Introduce new vocabulary words to describe what the children are doing and seeing (e.g., *So when the ramp is steeper, it makes the cars go down faster*).
- Encourage children to plan and predict their actions (e.g., ask the children how high they will pile the blocks at either end of the bridge, how long a plank they think they will need, and so on).
- Encourage children to make ramps of different heights and compare how far the cars go. Ask children if they want help measuring the heights and/ or writing down what they discover.

28 Exploring Nest-making Materials

Children use grass, straw, and other materials to build a bird's nest.

Time of day: Small-Group Time   **Content Area:** Science and Technology

Materials

Materials for each child and teacher:

- "Nest-making" materials such as grasses, straw, twigs, feathers, string, small strips of newspaper
- Firm mud or soft clay
- Strong piece of cardboard as a base

Shared materials:

- Bird's nest (more than one if possible)
- Chart paper and markers

Backup materials:

- Leaves

Beginning

- Briefly share the story of how you found the bird's nest. For example, you might say, *Joe, the groundskeeper, found this empty bird's nest in our tree. The birds grew up and flew away.*
- Encourage children to look at the nest and share their observations. Talk with them about the nest's size, shape, texture, thickness, and other properties. Write down children's observations.
- Distribute the materials and say something like *I wonder what you can do with these.*

Middle

- Watch and comment on how children are using the materials. Talk with them about the similarities between elements of their own nests and the properties of the bird's nest.

- Refocus children if necessary by adding backup materials or drawing their attention back to the bird's nest.

End

- Suggest a place that children can put their nests to dry. Put a work-in-progress sign on nests that children want to continue working on the next day.
- While children are cleaning up the materials and washing their hands, talk to them about how long they think it will take for the nests to dry.
- Suggest that children "fly like birds" to the next part of their day.

Ideas for follow-up

- Add books about birds and nests to the book area.
- Suggest that children look for more nests outside.
- Add other nest-building materials to the art area.
  [Note: Leaves and stems from dried herbs will add an extra sensory experience.]

Adaptations for children with special needs

- Encourage children with visual limitations to touch and feel the bird's nest; talk with them about its shape, texture, and other properties. Ask children to compare the feel of the materials used by the bird to make its nest to the materials they are using to build their own nests.

Developmental range: Supporting children at different levels

Earlier ⟶ **Middle** ⟶ **Later** ⟶

Earlier	Middle	Later
Children may	***Children may***	***Children may***
• Poke, squeeze, and pound the mud.	• Say, *I'm going to make a nest* and form a nestlike shape.	• Form a nestlike shape (base and walls) whose sides collapse; experiment with different materials as they problem-solve (e.g., discover that adding straw and twig pieces helps hold the nest together).
• Stick the straw (or other materials) into the mud.	• Stick the other materials around the outside and inside of their nest after looking at the bird's nest.	
• Form the mud into a shape; look at it and call it *my nest*.	• Comment on the materials they are using and how they compare to those of the bird's nest (e.g., *Mine has straw just like the bird's nest*).	• Pat the mud and the grasses together and then form it into a nestlike shape.
Adults can	• Pretend their fingers are birds that fly into their nest.	• Describe the nest-building process (e.g., *I'm mixing the mud and the straw all around the outside*).
• Imitate children's actions.	***Adults can***	• Lay feathers in the bottom of the nest *to make it soft for the eggs.*
• Ask children why they think birds like grass and straw in their nests.	• Comment on and compare actions of child and bird (e.g., *You're using your hands in the mud. Birds don't have hands. I wonder what birds use to build their nests with mud*). Listen to and accept child's explanations.	***Adults can***
• Acknowledge the nest the child made and comment that it looks like a nice place to lay eggs.	• Encourage children to talk about the materials they are using and their nest-building process.	• Comment on the children's problem-solving sequence (e.g., *First you tried just mud, then you added some string, and finally the walls of your nest stayed up when you used pieces of the twigs*).
	• Create another bird with their fingers and join the children's pretend bird in the nest. Ask children how the birds know that the nest is ready to move into. Accept the children's responses.	• Ask children how they think birds choose the materials for their nest.
		• Ask the children to estimate how long they think it takes for eggs to hatch into baby birds.

29 How Long Is a Minute?

Children march in place for one minute (as the teacher times them with a stopwatch or other device), then explore concepts related to measuring and estimating units of time.

Time of day: Small-Group Time

Content Area: Science and Technology

Materials

Materials for each child and teacher:

- None

Shared materials:

- A watch or timer with a stopwatch function (if possible, one with an audible tick)
- Chart paper and markers (one color for each child)

Backup materials:

- Other timing devices (e.g., one-minute sand timer, kitchen timer)

Beginning

- Show the stopwatch to the children and say *This is a stopwatch. It measures how long it takes to do something.*
- Ask children a series of "how long does it take" questions: *How long does it take you to put on your shoes? How long does it take you to get to school? How long does it take you to eat your snack?* Record children's answers on chart paper and discuss them as a group.
- Ask the children to think of other daily activities they routinely engage in and to guess how long these activities take. Record and discuss children's answers.
- Say *Lets find out how long a minute is. March in place until you think one minute has passed. I'll time you and we'll write down how long each of you marches.* Let each child choose a colored marker. Write their names and record how long they each march in seconds. Encourage children to write or copy their own names (or letter links) and their recorded time. Talk with them about how many seconds each one marched

and who marched a full minute, more or less than one minute, a longer or shorter time, and so on.

Middle

- Ask them to once again march in place but this time to continue marching until you tell them one minute or sixty seconds has passed. Repeat as you count out sixty seconds. [Note: You or the children can choose any quiet stationary movement that allows them to focus on the amount of time rather than the movement itself.]

Timing devices in the classroom, such as this one-minute sand timer, support children's developing sense of time and the units used to measure it.

- Discuss with the children how long they think one minute is, for example, a minute is how long it takes to do _____.
- Share other minute timers (e.g., sand timer, kitchen timer) and let children explore them. If your classroom has a clock with a second hand, point out that when that hand gets back to the numeral where it started, it means one minute has passed.

End

- Give a one-minute warning before the activity ends. Ask the children how they want to measure the minute (e.g., with the stopwatch, sand timer, wall clock).
- Together with the children, put away the chart pad and markers. Remind them where the stopwatch, sand timer, and any other timing devices are kept should they want to use them at work/choice time.
- Tell the children to walk around the room for a minute and then go to the next activity. Station yourself at the next activity; as children arrive let them know how close their time was to a minute.

Ideas for follow-up

- Play musical chairs (without winners and losers; there are enough chairs for each child, chairs are not removed, and each child plays every round). Stop the music after one minute.
- At large-group time, have children do movements (e.g., jump, walk, slide, bounce) for one minute and for other time lengths (e.g., one

second, ten seconds, two minutes). Talk about what it is like to do something for longer and shorter periods of time.
- Discuss in class a particular activity or routine children do at home (e.g., brush their teeth, put on their shoes, travel to school). Ask parents to help children time and record how long it takes them to do the activity/routine at home and to send the information back to class for discussion and comparison.
- Take photos of children performing activities in the classroom, and write below the photos the length of time (how many minutes) it took children to do the activities. Post the photos below or next to the relevant segment(s) of the daily routine chart.

Adaptations for children with special needs

- For children with physical limitations, suggest activities they can perform using wheelchairs (e.g., wheel around the table, tap their hands on their trays) or other assistive devices. Encourage children to talk about whether it takes more or less time to accomplish certain tasks (e.g., longer time to get dressed but shorter time to wheel across the room compared to someone who is walking).
- For children with visual limitations, use timers that make noise (e.g., clocks that tick the seconds loudly).
- For children with auditory limitations, use timers that show the passage of seconds (e.g., clocks with large second hands).

Developmental range: Supporting children at different levels

Earlier →

Children may

- Respond *I don't know* when asked to estimate how long everyday activities take.
- Estimate time in general terms rather than in standard units (e.g., *a long time; I do that real quick*).
- Stop long before one minute has passed (e.g., after five to ten seconds) during a timed activity.
- Pause during a timed activity (e.g., marching for one minute) and start again.

Adults can

- Encourage children to guess how long familiar activities take.
- Use general time-related language (e.g., *It takes longer to walk to the corner than it does to walk to the door; You eat one pretzel in less time than you eat five pretzels*).
- Use specific vocabulary words related to units of time (e.g., *seconds, minutes, hours*).
- Point out when children march for less/more/same amount of time as one minute (e.g., *You stopped, but the stopwatch is still going; The sand timer is done, but you're still marching; You stopped at exactly the same time as the stopwatch! You both went for one minute*).
- Say numerals aloud as you write and read them.

Middle →

Children may

- State answers in standard time units but do so incorrectly (e.g., *It takes my mom 10 minutes and 10 hours to drive me to school; I brush my teeth for eleventy-eight seconds*).
- Vary widely in or exaggerate their estimates (e.g., *fast like a second; a billion minutes*).
- Look at peers to decide whether to stop, continue, or resume marching.
- Recognize and name written numerals on the chart paper and/or timers.
- Say who marched longer, shorter, or the same amount of time.

Adults can

- Make statements using standard time units correctly (e.g., *I drive to school in 15 minutes; My dentist said I should brush my teeth for one minute. That's 60 seconds*).
- Ask children to march for one second, five seconds, ten seconds. Count the seconds aloud with them. Discuss the comparative quickness of a second versus a minute.
- Ask children to compare their estimate of a minute (e.g., 20 seconds) vs. 60 seconds on the stopwatch. Ask *Which is longer, 20 seconds or 60 seconds?*
- Help children connect (benchmark) one minute to something concrete (e.g., when they tire, sweat, get bored).
- Encourage children to read the numerals on the chart paper and timers/clocks.

Later →

Children may

- State answers in reasonably correct standard time units (e.g., *Snacktime is for 10 minutes; We leave the house a half-hour before school starts; I can walk across the room in 10 seconds*).
- Connect (benchmark) the length of a minute with something they know (e.g., count and march to 100).
- Look at a timer (e.g., wall clock, sand timer, stopwatch) teacher is holding to decide whether to stop, continue, or resume jumping.
- Compare how long different activities take (e.g., *Brushing my teeth takes longer than tying my shoe; It takes a whole hour to get to grandma's but only a minute to drive to school*).

Adults can

- Connect standard time units to one another (e.g., *If it takes 60 minutes to drive to your dad's house, that makes an hour*).
- Help children connect (benchmark) one minute to something quantitative (e.g., the sweep of the second hand), counting slowly to 60.
- Encourage children to compare different types of minute timers (e.g., simultaneously start the stopwatch and turn over the one-minute sand timer). Help them observe that a minute is the same no matter how it is measured.
- Ask children to compare time lengths in quantitative terms (e.g., *How many more seconds did the watch go after you stopped marching?*).
- Encourage children to copy or write numerals.

30 Ice Cubes and Trays

Children explore ice cubes, watching them melt and making observations of and predictions about the process.

Time of day: Small-Group Time

Content Area: Science and Technology

Materials

Materials for each child and teacher:

- Ice cubes — at least 2
- Plastic trays (e.g., lunch trays, empty and clean frozen dinner trays)

Shared materials:

- None

Backup materials:

- Extra ice cubes

Beginning

- Say something related to children's previous experiences with melting ice and/or snow (e.g., *Yesterday we wondered why nearly all the icicles had melted from the edge of the roof. Maybe it was the sun, or Joe banged them off, or they just slipped off the edge*).
- Demonstrate "skating" an ice cube around on a tray. Talk with the children about how the ice cube moves, leaves a trail of water, melts/shrinks, and so on.
- Give each child a tray and two ice cubes and say, *I have some trays and ice cubes for you. I wonder if you'll come up with some more ideas about what makes the ice melt.*

Middle

- Talk with the children about what they are doing. Encourage them to describe their actions and what they see happening to the ice.
- Listen to the words they use (e.g., *melt, slip; cold, wet; It's turning into water!*), and add new vocabulary words related to the attributes of the cubes and the melting process (e.g., *shrink, slide, glide; bigger/smaller, before/after, all gone; trail of water, squiggly wet line*).

End

- Dump the leftover ice cubes in the water table (or a plastic basin). Tell children they can check on the ice cubes after the next activity. Ask them to predict what will happen.
- Ask the children to "skate" to the next part of the daily routine.

Ideas for follow-up

- Add ice cubes to the water table at work/choice time the next day. Ask children to predict what they think the water table will look like at the end of the activity. Provide tape (or other markers) if children want to mark the water level at different points. Repeat this activity giving each child two baskets, one with tiny cups of salt. Encourage them to compare the rate at which ice cubes melt with and without salt.
- At outside time or during a neighborhood walk, observe and talk about melting ice and snow with the children. For example, compare the amount of time it takes for ice/snow to melt in sunny and shady areas, on sidewalks where there is more/less pedestrian traffic, and so on. Talk about what happens when ice melts and refreezes. Encourage children to describe what they see and explain why they think it is happening.
- Take photographs of melting ice cubes and put them like puzzle pieces in the toy area, where children can put them in order.
- Use ice cubes as "paintbrushes" with dry tempera and construction paper.

Adaptations for children with special needs

- Have mittens available for children who have sensory (tactile) issues.
- Encourage children with visual limitations to explore the tactile properties of the ice cubes and the melting process (e.g., to feel the difference between a solid cube and a watery [melting] one; to feel temperature differences as the ice cube turns to water).

Teachers can begin this activity by talking with children about their experiences with snow and ice at outside time and what they've observed about the melting process.

Developmental range: Supporting children at different levels

Earlier ⟶   **Middle** ⟶   **Later** ⟶

Earlier

Children may

- Move the ice around the tray and make "motor" noises.
- Observe that the ice cube "disappeared" (e.g., *Mrs. Ewing, my ice is gone!*).
- Exclaim how the ice feels on their fingers (e.g., *Hey, this is really cold!*).
- Tip their tray to make the melting ice move back and forth, closely watching the water stream.

Adults can

- Watch how children are using the materials and make comments about what children are doing (e.g., *Ben, you're moving your ice all over the whole tray*).
- Call the child's attention to the melting process (e.g., *Jasmine, your ice cube was bigger just a minute ago. Now I see mostly water on your tray!*).
- Try using the materials in the same way the child does (e.g., *Rosa, my ice cube moves really fast when I tip my tray the same way you are doing*).

Middle

Children may

- Notice the ice cube has melted (e.g., *Hey, mine's all melted! I need another one!*).
- Use their ice cube to "draw" on their tray.
- Try to "race" two ice cubes on their tray by tilting it from one side to another.

Adults can

- Repeat children's words and add new words associated with melting; (e.g., *You've rubbed the ice with your warm fingers and now all you have left is a puddle of water*).
- Ask children to describe what they have done with the ice (e.g., *Can you tell me about the designs you are making with the melted ice?*).
- Ask children to predict which ice cube will "win the race" and why.
- Encourage children to come up with explanations for what they see happening (e.g., *I wonder why ice cubes slide*).

Later

Children may

- Comment on what happens when the ice cube is melting (e.g., *My ice is leaving a water trail*).
- Come to a conclusion about why the ice is melting (e.g., *The ice is leaking all over the place. The faster it moves, the more it melts*).
- Hold their ice cubes in their hands to make them melt faster (e.g., *Nani, if we hold them tight, they'll melt faster*).

Adults can

- Use sequence words to describe the melting process (e.g., First *you had the ice,* next *you moved it on your tray, and* now *you just have water*).
- Ask children why they think the ice melted. Accept their explanations and encourage them to elaborate (e.g., *Why do you think it melts faster when it moves?*).
- Pose a question about slowing down the melting process (e.g., *So if you hold your ice cube in both hands, it melts faster. What could I do to make my ice cube last longer?*).

31 Painting With Corn Syrup and Food Coloring

Children mix corn syrup with food coloring to create designs and observe the effects of different combinations of materials.

Materials

Materials for each child and teacher:
- Large piece of wax paper
- Small paper cups (half full) of corn syrup
- Paintbrush
- Squeeze bottle of food coloring
- Basket or similar container

Shared materials:
- None

Backup materials:
- Cardboard (to use as a base when transferring paintings to a drying place)
- Extra pieces of wax paper
- Extra squeeze bottles of food coloring

Beginning
- While showing the children a cup of corn syrup, say *Today I have something different to paint with. It's thick and sticky. It's called corn syrup.*
- Give each child a basket of materials and say *I wonder how it will look and feel when you paint with these.*

Middle
- Use the materials yourself and imitate the children's actions.
- Describe and comment on what children are doing with the paintbrush. Repeat their words and introduce new vocabulary words (e.g., *You are* pushing *your corn syrup with the brush; You are* swirling *the corn syrup around by* making big circles; *You are making* up-and-down *and* side-to-side brush strokes *on your wax paper; You are* pouring *your syrup onto the wax paper.*
- As children continue to work or start losing interest, introduce the food coloring. Give each child one small squeeze bottle and say *I have some food coloring and I am wondering what will happen when you add it to your painting of the corn syrup.* If children did not get a color they wanted, help them to problem-solve (e.g., *Maybe you could ask someone to trade with you*).
- Talk with the children about what they think their pictures will look like when they dry. Explain that it will take a few days for the corn syrup to dry but that they can check on the pictures each day to see what is happening.

End
- Have children decide on the best place for their pictures to dry. Place the wax paper on the cardboard because the corn syrup and coloring will be runny and the pictures will be difficult to carry. [Note: you may want to have extra paper towels for the children to blot off the extra food coloring before moving them.]
- After children wash their hands, ask them to move as if they "have corn syrup on their shoes" to the next part of the day.

Ideas for follow-up
- Have children check to see what is happening with the corn syrup as it dries. (Corn syrup will get shiny and smooth. If moved, it will wrinkle. If the corn syrup is exposed to cold tempera-

tures, it will crack; when exposed to warm temperatures, it will turn back to being shiny and smooth.)

- Once the pictures are thoroughly dry, ask children what they think about being able to see through their picture. Hold up your picture and have children look through the corn syrup and colors. Point out that you might be able to see through some areas that are thin but not through the thick areas. Have them look at their own pictures and converse about what they see with their pictures (e.g., *You can see through your red color but it is black in this spot; Look how thin it is on this side and how thick the* *corn syrup and color is over here*). Give children flashlights and let them shine the flashlights under their pictures to discover the different colors made by the food coloring.
- Combine the corn syrup with regular paint for another small-group time.

Adaptations for children with special needs

- Provide large brushes for children with manual coordination difficulties, and/or encourage them to paint with their hands.
- Offer plastic gloves to children concerned about working with "sticky" materials.

Developmental range: Supporting children at different levels

Earlier ——→	Middle ——→	Later ——→

Children may

- Pour syrup onto the paper and swirl or push it with the brush.
- Talk about how the corn syrup feels and looks (e.g., *It's sticky; Look, mine's dripping; Hey, this is cool*).
- Use their fingers instead of the paintbrush.
- Watch what the syrup is doing as they move it around with the paintbrush.
- Fill (or not fill) the paper; ask for more syrup and/or paper.

Adults can

- Imitate children's actions by using the corn syrup and food coloring.
- Describe what children do with the syrup and food coloring (e.g., *Look at the colors you are making when you mix them with the corn syrup; You're pouring the syrup in one place and it is getting thick*).
- Encourage children to describe how it feels to use the materials (e.g., *I wonder what it feels like when you dab your brush in the syrup*).
- Encourage children to use additional materials and to try different actions and effects.

Children may

- Make purposeful actions with the paintbrush to get the design they want (e.g., *This time I'm going to smoosh it all around so it fills the whole page!*).
- Describe what they are doing and making with the materials (e.g., *I'm making syrup and pancakes; I'm making bubbles; Look, mine's getting thick and hers is running on the table*).
- Talk about the effect of adding food coloring (*Now it's got color. I made it red!*).

Adults can

- Talk with children about the different effects they can create with the corn syrup (e.g., *What do you think happens when you put the corn syrup on the wax paper?; Look at the beads you make when you spread the syrup over the wax paper; What do you think would happen if you held your brush up and let the corn syrup fall back onto the wax paper?*).
- Describe and encourage children to describe the effects they observe (e.g., *When you added red to the corn syrup, it made streaks; I wonder what made the bubbles*).
- Encourage children's representations and role playing (e.g., *Those pancakes and syrup look yummy! You're making a lot of them*).

Children may

- Show greater control over the media and manipulate them with intention (e.g., pour corn syrup and/or food coloring in specific spots on paper; repeat an action to get the same design or pattern).
- Talk about their actions and what they see happening with the corn syrup and food coloring (e.g., *I'm mixing blue and yellow to make green; Mine's real dark because I mixed all of the colors together*).
- Compare corn syrup to other materials they have painted with (e.g., *This is thicker than paint; It's smoother to brush than when we painted with paste*).

Adults can

- Refer children to one other and encourage them to try one another's ideas (e.g., *Aaron is scraping the corn syrup with his nails. I wonder what would happen if you tried scraping yours that way*).
- Encourage children to describe and explain their discoveries (e.g., *You noticed how the corn syrup spreads out when you pour it in one place. Why do you suppose that happens?*).
- Talk about the designs and patterns children are making (e.g., *Your corn syrup is making a row of dots when you spread it across your paper; You made a pattern — blue, clear, blue, clear, blue, clear*).
- Talk with children about other painting materials and tools they have used; encourage them to compare the actions and results of different combinations of materials.

32 Pots, Pans, and Cans — Oh, My!

Children produce sounds with different combinations of assorted materials.

Time of day: Small-Group Time   **Content Area:** Science and Technology

Materials

Materials for each child and teacher:

- Assorted items to bang (e.g., pots, pans, lids, large juice cans, gallon milk jugs, clapperless bells of various sizes, tuning fork); gather these in a large basket, tub, or trash can outside, or have children help you carry them outside at the beginning of small-group time
- Strikers (e.g., mallets with soft and hard ends, wooden and metal spoons, rhythm sticks, rigid plastic rod) — at least 2–3 for each child
- Bucket (large enough to hold assorted strikers)

Shared materials:

- None

Backup materials:

- Variety of items for banging on, tied to or suspended from a fence (e.g., bells, triangles, thin and thick wooden blocks, leather straps)

Beginning

- Say something like *I went to a concert last night and the musicians were banging drums and all kinds of things to make different sounds.*
- Give each child a bucket with assorted strikers and say *Today we are having small-group time outside so we can make plenty of noise.* (If necessary, move outside at this point). *In your bucket, you'll find things you can use to bang with to make noise. These* [point to pans, bells, etc.] *are different things you can bang on.*

Middle

- Observe and listen carefully, distinguishing between distinct, purposeful sounds and random pounding.

- Be aware of those children who are sensitive to loud noise and who may want to move away from the group to where the sounds are not as loud.
- As you move around, watch and listen for indications from the children that they detect differences in the sounds they are producing (e.g., they may comment on differences in loudness or tone; systematically alternate two sounds and cock their head to listen).
- Encourage children to describe what they are doing and hearing.
- Support their efforts by making an occasional *I wonder …* statement or a *What do you think would happen if …?* question.
- Listen for indications that some of the children not only hear a sound but feel something; they might describe it as "tickling." This is an opportunity to scaffold children's learning by introducing the idea that sound is made up of vibrations and the tickling they feel is a result of those vibrations. You can show them other ways (e.g., putting fingers on their vocal chords) to feel sound vibrations.

End

- Together with the children, sort the objects according to the area of the room where they are usually stored. Remind children they can use them again at work/choice time or outside time.
- Encourage children to imitate one of the sounds they made as they move to the next activity.

Ideas for follow-up

- Suspend additional items that are weather tolerant from outside fences to give children more opportunities to explore different sounds at outside time (e.g., small garden tools made of wood, plastic, or metal; sandbox toys; hoses; buckets filled with different materials or left empty).
- At planning (and recall) time, make available to children objects labeled with different area signs. Children can use a striker to select an object labeled with the sign of the classroom area where they would like to play (or did play) and then talk about what they plan to do there (or what they did).

Adaptations for children with special needs

- Encourage children who are bothered by loud noises to select an "instrument" with a gentler sound (e.g., a triangle, bamboo or wooden sticks) and to find a place removed from most of the noise.
- For children with hearing difficulties, include object-striker combinations that produce vibrations they can feel.

Developmental range: Supporting children at different levels

Earlier ⟶   **Middle** ⟶   **Later** ⟶

Children may

- Consistently bang on one item with the same striker (e.g., bang on a pot with a spoon; bang on the milk jug with the soft mallet).
- Randomly hit different objects with different strikers; try all or most of the objects and strikers.
- Say they are making a noise.

Adults can

- Play alongside children, using the same objects and strikers children choose and imitating their gestures.
- Acknowledge that the child is making different sounds. Comment about a particular sound or respond to a comment the child makes (e.g., *Yes, that was a loud noise*).
- Wonder what sounds would be made by specific combinations (e.g., *I wonder how it would sound if you used this stick with that block*).

Children may

- Compare the sounds made by two strikers on the same object or by the same striker on two different objects (e.g., strike a piece of bamboo with a rhythm stick and then with another piece of bamboo; use the mallet to strike the triangle and then a wooden block).
- Listen intently to the sounds they make (e.g., put their ear closer to hear and stand very still).
- Comment on the sound they make (e.g., clap two pot lids together and say, *These are like cymbals in the marching band*).

Adults can

- Comment on and encourage children to compare two sound effects (e.g., *Those don't sound the same. How do you think they sound different?*).
- Ask why the child thinks an object or striker produces a particular effect (e.g., *You said hitting two pieces of bamboo together makes a sound like tock. I wonder why it makes that sound*).
- Ask children to predict what an object-striker combination will sound like (e.g., *What do you think would happen if you hit the cowbell with your palm?*).
- Enter into the children's role playing, following their lead (e.g., ask to join their marching band).

Children may

- Systematically compare the sound effects of different strikers on one or more objects (e.g., try each type of striker on a triangle hanging from a tree branch, then try different strikers on a pot).
- Explore what happens when objects are hit in different positions (e.g., striking a triangle when it is suspended or lying flat on the ground).
- Describe and compare two or more sounds (e.g., *It's louder when I use the metal bar than when I use the stick*).
- Describe the physical sensation of striking objects (e.g., hit the big cowbell hard with one of the soft mallets and say, *I feel tickles up my arm*; hit the tuning fork on the edge of a pan, hold it up to his/her jaw, and say, *I can feel something in my bones*).

Adults can

- Encourage children to describe and compare the sound effects of different object-striker combinations (e.g., *What kind of a sound is a thunky one? Can you show me something that makes a different kind of sound?*).
- Encourage children to explore sound effects when objects are in different positions or hit in different ways (e.g., *I wonder how it would sound if you put it on the grass?*).
- Ask children to explain how they created particular sounds or sensations (e.g., *Show me what you did so I can make my arm tickle too*).

33 Shadows: Now They're Here, Now They're Not

Children stand/move behind a sheet, exploring the effects of different light patterns and creating shadows.

Time of day: Small-Group Time   **Content Area:** Science and Technology

Materials

Materials for each child and teacher:

- None

Shared materials:

- Large window to act as a light source
- A sheet or other sheer piece of fabric to hang in front of the window

Backup materials:

- A collection of props from the house area that children can wear to make interesting shadows (e.g., hats, wigs, scarves, jackets, tall boots, mittens).

Beginning

- Say something like *Do you remember when we went for a walk the other day and sometimes our shadows were there and sometimes they disappeared? Why do you think that happened?* Talk with the children about their ideas.
- Stand between the window and the sheet and ask the children to describe what they see. Then step back out and talk with the children about what they see now. Discuss whether/ where they saw a shadow, when/how it disappeared, what it looked like (e.g., in what ways did it look like you or not), and so on.
- Encourage the children to work in pairs so they can take turns standing behind the sheet and reporting on what they see.

Middle

- Encourage children who are standing behind the sheet to move in different ways.

- Encourage children who are observing to describe the shadows they see (e.g., fuzzy, dancing, tall, small; shadows with flapping arms).
- Ask for children's ideas on what they think is happening (i.e., what does or does not make a shadow appear and disappear).
- Introduce the props from the house area and tell children they might like to try making different kinds of shadow.

End

- Have each child pass behind the sheet on their way to the next activity. Describe the shadows you see them make as they pass by.

As a follow-up to this activity, teachers can add flashlights to the classroom so that children can experiment with the effects of light and shadow.

- Ask children for ideas about where in the classroom to store the sheet so they can use it again at work/choice time if they choose.

Ideas for follow-up

- Do a similar activity at small-group time, introducing the idea of shadow puppets. Give each child a basket containing scissors, cardstock, tape, and tongue depressors to make their own shadow puppets. (Begin by demonstrating how to make a shadow puppet with two to three materials.)
- Try shadow play outside on partly sunny days. Talk with the children about when they do or do not see shadows, depending on the amount and position of the sun.
- Observe the effects of light and shade on the shadows cast by playground equipment and natural objects (e.g., trees, plant stalks).
- Point out when changing light patterns affect the presence and absence of shadows in the classroom.

- Add flashlights to the classroom along with paper and fabric of different thicknesses so children can experiment with light and shadow effects.

Adaptations for children with special needs

- Assist children using wheelchairs, walkers, or other equipment in going behind the sheet. Encourage their peers to describe the shadows they see (e.g., the wheelchair, the person in the chair, the person pushing the chair, the turning spokes on the wheelchair).
- For children who have visual limitations but who can see light and dark, exaggerate visual effects by using more powerful lights behind the sheet (e.g., hold a lamp or flashlight behind the sheet so the child with the visual impairment can see the effects).

Developmental range: Supporting children at different levels

Earlier →

Children may
- Say they do (or do not) see a shadow.
- Stand behind the sheet and say, *Hey I can't see a shadow from back here.*
- Ask the teacher or another child, *Can you see my shadow now? How about now?*
- Say whether the shadow is standing still or moving.

Adults can
- Move behind and in front of the sheet and ask children if they can see a shadow.
- Move in different ways behind the sheet and ask children to say what they see.
- Encourage children to move in different ways behind the sheet and tell them how they look; use different words to describe children's motions (e.g., *I can see from your shadow that you are bending down*).
- Encourage children to work in pairs and to describe their actions to each other.

Middle →

Children may
- Take turns with another child. Describe to one another what they see.
- Imitate the movements of the teacher or another child behind the sheet.
- Ask another child to imitate their actions so they can see what it looks like (e.g., *I want a turn watching. Do the same thing so I can see what it looks like*).
- Pretend to be something, like a giant taking huge steps back and forth in front of the window. Describe what they are doing and ask other(s) what it looks like (e.g., *I'm taking giant steps. Tell me what you see!*).

Adults can
- Ask children to explain their movements and imitate them.
- Encourage children to take turns being the leader (e.g., one child does a shadow movement behind the sheet, then others get behind the sheet and try to do the same thing). Encourage the leader to use position and direction words to describe the movement.
- Acknowledge children's role playing. Ask questions such as *How does a giant move? Does a giant look different behind or in front of a sheet? How could you find out? Oops, your giant just got smaller. Why do you think that happened?*

Later →

Children may
- Systematically vary their movements and ask others about the effects (e.g., move their hand a little, a bit more, then a lot and ask what the other person sees).
- Speculate about what does (or does not) make a shadow (e.g., *You have to be behind the sheet — if you're in front, the shadow is gone*).
- Talk about what does (or does not) make shadows at other times (e.g., *You only see shadows when the sun is shining*).
- Make shadows with props and describe and compare the effects (e.g., *When I put on the fireman's mitt, my hand makes a big ball. My shadow doesn't have fingers!*).

Adults can
- Vary position(s) behind the sheet (e.g., close to the window, up against the sheet) and ask children to describe what they see. Encourage children to explain the reason for the differences they see.
- Accept and talk about children's ideas related to what does (or does not) make a shadow (e.g., *What if your back is close to the window but not touching it? Would that make a shadow?*).
- Talk about the props children use and the shadows these create; encourage children to compare the prop (when it's not behind the sheet) to its shadow.
- Ask children to make (or explain how to make) specific effects (e.g., *I wonder how you could make a short shadow; Suppose I wanted to make my shadow really big, what should I do?*).

34 Squeeze and Blow

Children fill squeezable items with air and "blow" objects of various weights and sizes, comparing differences in how fast (speed) and how far (distance) the objects travel.

Time of day: Small-Group Time

Content Area: Science and Technology

Materials

Materials for each child and teacher:
- Squeeze bottles and turkey basters
- Feathers

Shared materials:
- None

Backup materials:
- Objects of different sizes, weights, and density (e.g., ping-pong balls, tissues, ribbons; small rubber balls, heavier weight paper, cotton socks)
- Conventional and unconventional measuring tools (e.g., rulers, tape measures; string, blocks)

Beginning

- Tell the children a story, for example, *Once upon a time there was a teeny-tiny dog who had a teeny-tiny boat with a teeny-tiny sail. One day the dog went out for a sail on the not-so-teeny-tiny lake. The wind stopped and the dog was stuck in the middle of the lake with no wind to blow him home. What do you think he decided to do?* Talk with the children about their ideas. Then say *Well, he decided to see if he could blow on the sail to get him home.*
- Give each child a set of materials and say *Here are some materials that you can use to pretend you're trying to get a boat across a lake.*

Middle

- Observe and imitate children's actions as they use squeeze devices to try to move the feather and other objects. Ask them to describe what they did so you can copy them. Talk about whether you did (or did not) get the same results they did.

- Repeat children's words as they describe what's happening, and introduce new vocabulary words related to air (e.g., *whoosh, breeze, big wind, puffs*) and speed (e.g., *faster/slower*).
- Encourage children to experiment with the different squeezers by filling them with air and blowing objects on different surfaces (e.g., tabletop, water table, rug).
- Introduce the masking tape *in case you want to mark out a space for your lake or a finish line for a race, or anything else.*
- Introduce additional objects, encouraging children to compare the effects of different squeezers and different surfaces on the movement of those objects.
- For children who are interested in counting, help them count (and tally) the number of squeezes it takes to move an object a given distance, such as across a carpet square. For those interested in measuring, help them measure how far the objects travel under different conditions (blowing on objects with different squeezers and on different surfaces).

End

- Ask children to move "like feathers being blown by the wind" to the next activity.
- Remind children where the materials are stored should they want to experiment or continue their racing game at work/choice time.

Ideas for follow-up

- Add other squeeze devices (e.g., bellows, paper fans) and objects (e.g., large hollow balls, cylindrical blocks) to the classroom (e.g., in the house area or at the water table).
- If children create and write rules for a "race," ask them if they want to post the rules so they can continue to play their game at work time.

- Repeat the activity using water as well as air to fill the squeezers. Encourage children to compare the effects on speed and distance traveled of using different objects and squeezers and the two types of fillers.

Adaptations for children with special needs

- For children with motor difficulties who find it hard to squeeze or blow, ask them to tell you or another child which action to perform for them. Ask them to talk about what they see happening.

- Encourage children with visual impairments to use their other senses to feel what they may have trouble seeing. For example, you might blow air against their cheek using a variety of squeeze devices and let them feel and compare the differences.

Developmental range: Supporting children at different levels

Earlier ———————————▶

Children may

- Ask how to use the baster (e.g., *How do I get this thing to work?*).
- Explore the movement of the feather without using the baster or squeeze bottle (e.g., *My feather keeps trying to float away, it won't stay still*).
- Use their breath to blow on the feathers (e.g., *Just blow them with your own air*).

Adults can

- Demonstrate how to use the baster. Refer children to one another for help (e.g., *Maybe Heidi can show you how she got the baster to work*).
- Talk to children about the movement of the feather and the effect of children's actions on its speed. Encourage children to describe and explain what they observe (e.g., *How did you make it move faster?; What happened when you pushed it?; I wonder why it stopped*).
- Imitate the children's actions. Ask children to describe what they did (e.g., *How should I blow on my feather to make it move like yours?*).

Middle ———————————▶

Children may

- Comment on or compare which type of squeezer is easier to use (e.g., *Try the squeeze bottles; they're not so hard*).
- Play a game of racing their feathers (e.g., *Let's have a race across the floor, both using squeeze bottles*).
- Compare the distance traveled and/or speed of feathers (e.g., *Wow, look how far ours went on the tile. They went farthest of all*).
- Try to make a variety of other objects move (e.g., *I can't make the rubber balls go. They're too heavy!*).

Adults can

- Acknowledge children's observations and comments; ask if they can explain what they see (e.g., *Why do you think the squeeze bottle is easier to use?; Show me what you did with the baster; Why is it so hard to move the rubber ball?*).
- Ask children how they will set up their race to know which feather reached the end first. Encourage them to race on different surfaces (e.g., tabletop, rug, water table) and to try different squeezers. Talk to them about the results (e.g., *So you think the feather went faster on the table because the table is smooth, but it went slower on the rug because it got caught in the loops*).
- Repeat children's words and introduce new vocabulary words (e.g., *It went* fastest *when you blew on it; Which squeezer makes it go farthest?; Mine went the* shortest *distance and yours went the* longest *across the table*).

Later ———————————▶

Children may

- Comment on how the squeezers work (e.g., *If you suck air into the turkey thing and then squeeze it on the feather, it goes farther than if you just blow!*).
- Establish simple "rules" for a race (e.g., *Okay, put the tape down there so we have a finish line. Then we have to say,* Ready-Set-Go, *and we have to count how many squeezes it takes to get to the finish line*).
- Systematically compare squeezers and comment on the results (e.g., *I did them* both [bottle and baster]. *The best is the baster when you squeeze it really hard and fast*).

Adults can

- Encourage children to explain what they observe (e.g., *I wonder why squeezing with the turkey baster worked better than when you just blew on the feather*).
- Ask children to predict what will happen when they use different squeezers to blow objects on different surfaces.
- Talk with children about the rules they create for their race or other game(s). Ask if they want help writing them down.
- Encourage and help children who are interested to count the number of squeezes or blows it takes to move an object.
- Encourage and help children who are interested to measure how far the feathers and other objects travel with different squeeze techniques and on different surfaces.

35 What's in a Ball?

Children use assorted tools to take apart a variety of balls and explore their inside and outside properties.

Time of day: Small-Group Time   **Content Area:** Science and Technology

Materials

Materials for each child and teacher:

- 2 or more balls of different types (e.g., softballs, baseballs, tennis balls). Split the balls apart (except for the one you are going to demonstrate with) ahead of time
- 2 or more tools for taking apart the balls (e.g., tweezers, forks, scissors, pliers)

Shared materials:

- None

Backup materials:

- Assortment of balls (e.g., solid rubber, ping-pong, foam, golf)
- Tools for taking apart the balls

Beginning

- Talk with the children about the different types of balls they have played with. Say *I sometimes wonder what's inside the balls.* Talk to the children about their ideas of what is inside different types of balls.
- Using the various tools, demonstrate how to open up a ball and take it apart. Talk to the children briefly about what they see inside.
- Give each child a basket and say *Here are a couple of types of balls that have already been split open. I wonder what is inside them.*

Middle

- Talk with the children about their actions as they use the tools. Ask them what they see inside the balls. Encourage them to experiment with different tools and techniques for using them. Support their problem-solving efforts and acknowledge/scaffold their observations.

- Repeat children's words and introduce new vocabulary related to the balls and their properties (e.g., *rough, dark, smooth, spongy, full/empty, soft/hard*), the tools children are using (e.g., *tweezers, pliers, prongs*), and the children's actions (e.g., *pick, slice, slit*).
- Give children whole balls they can take apart with the tools they have. Encourage children to find other tools from the classroom to take apart the balls.

End

- Together with the children, sort materials and tools. Remind children where these items will be stored should they want to continue using them at work/choice time.
- Ask children to "roll like balls" to the next activity.

Ideas for follow-up

- Have a tub of balls in the woodworking area where children can use a vise and different tools to take the balls apart and explore what's inside them. Suggest they leave some whole, partially peel others, and cut some in half or quarters.
- Provide other items children can take apart and explore, such as pillows or old wind-up clocks. Ask families to donate old items they no longer use to the classroom. Make sure items are safe (e.g., no sharp edges).

Adaptations for children with special needs

- Encourage children with visual limitations to feel and compare the insides of the balls. If necessary, help them remove the covers.

Developmental range: Supporting children at different levels

Earlier ——————→

Children may
- Bounce or roll the ball on the table.
- Poke their fingers into the slits adult has made in the balls.
- Try several times to peel off the outside of the ball; ask for help.
- Try another type of ball before getting the outside layer off the ball they tried first.
- Look at the inside of ball(s) whose outside cover another child has removed.

Adults can
- Comment on how the child is making the ball move.
- Encourage children to describe what they see and feel inside different balls.
- Encourage children to help one another remove ball covers (e.g., *Maybe Jason can show you how he got the cover off with his tweezers*).
- If children appear frustrated, suggest strategies for removing covers (e.g., *Sometimes when I have trouble getting the cover off, I put one hand on each side of the slit and pull it apart*).
- Provide extra balls that are partially peeled for children who are really struggling.

Middle ——————→

Children may
- Express surprise at what they discover inside the ball (e.g., *Whoa! It's weird when you take the skin off!*).
- Notice differences between balls (e.g., *Mine looks new, but Jerry's is old and dirty*).
- Use descriptive words to share their discoveries about the insides of the balls (e.g., *It looks like this has all rubber-bands inside. They're really stretchy!; This fuzzy yellow ball is smooth and empty inside like the plastic eggs!*).
- Try to put the balls back together.

Adults can
- Share children's sense of surprise and delight about their discoveries.
- Describe and encourage children to describe what they are doing and seeing (e.g., *China, you tugged until the cover came off. What do you see on the inside? How is it the same [or different] from the outside*).
- Use other descriptive words to extend the child's vocabulary (e.g., *firm, solid, rigid, flexible, stretchy*).
- Ask the child to predict if a different type of ball will look the same or different on the inside.

Later ——————→

Children may
- Once the outside cover of the ball is off, work through the other layers to see what's inside.
- Try a variety of tools; get tools from other areas of the classroom.
- Try to split apart other kinds of balls.
- Compare the properties of different balls and what's inside them (e.g., *This one is hard and that's soft; This ball is packed really full but this one not so much; The foam ball is the same on the inside and the outside!*).
- Describe their problem-solving efforts (e.g., *The fork didn't work, so I poked it with the tweezers*).

Adults can
- Ask children to predict if they will need a different tool to open up the second ball.
- Encourage children to describe their problem-solving efforts (e.g., *So first you tried the fork, next you tried pounding it on the table and that didn't work. What did you do then?*).
- Encourage children to use sequence words to describe what they did (e.g., *I see the cover is off your softball. Can you share what you did to take it apart? What did you do first?*).

V. The Arts: Visual Art & Music

The arts have been a standard feature of preschool programs since their beginning. Researcher Carol Seefeldt (1999) says that even during periods when educators are pressured to focus on other academic skills, such as reading, most continue to believe the arts should remain an essential component of the early childhood curriculum.

Research supports this enduring belief. Experiences in the arts benefit children throughout their school years. The value of artistic instruction for students is both emotional and intellectual. Art is *intrinsically rewarding,* that is, studying art is important for its own sake. For young children, in particular, art provides an inner sense of competence and control. The Task Force on Children's Learning and the Arts notes that "as they engage in the artistic process, children learn that they can observe, organize, and interpret their experiences.

They can make decisions, take actions, and monitor the effect of those actions" (Arts Education Partnership, 1998, p. 2).

Art is also *extrinsically valuable* in promoting other areas of development. "For all children, at all ability levels, the arts play a central role in cognitive, motor, language, and social-emotional development. The arts motivate and engage children in learning, stimulate memory and facilitate understanding, enhance symbolic communication, promote relationships, and provide an avenue for building competence" (AEP, 1998, p. v).

The developmental changes that occur in the preschool years make young children especially open to enjoying and learning from the opportunities that education in the arts presents. Preschoolers, as distinct from infants and toddlers, are able to form mental images. Their developing language skills open up new avenues for artistic expression,

Experiences in the arts are rewarding for their own sake. The arts also provide learning opportunities in cognition, language, motor development, and social-emotional skills.

for example, through describing what they see or hear in a work of visual or performance art, or through the verbal and written ideas in their own imaginative play. When their expanding cognitive capacities are combined with their growing physical and social abilities, preschoolers have a wide array of options for appreciating and creating in the arts. They can make drawings and build models, imitate and pretend, sing and invent the words to songs, and express themselves as adult artists do in ways that are consistent with their developmental levels and abilities.

Four principles, derived from child development research, guide HighScope's approach to early arts education (Epstein & Trimis, 2002):

- **Representation grows out of children's real experiences.** To form mental images, young children first need hands-on experiences with objects, people, and events. For example, when they play "mommy" and "baby," children carry out roles they typically see in their own families. Drawings and clay models reflect the people and objects they see in their everyday lives, as well as in books, toys, and electronic media. Children's melodies, rhythms, and song topics arise from their musical experiences at home and school.
- **Children's representations develop from the simple to the complex.** Whatever the medium (painting, acting, singing), children's representations begin simply and evolve in complexity with time and practice. Initially, children hold only one or two characteristics of an object, person, or event in mind. Later, as they are able to mentally store images with more attributes and use materials with more dexterity, their representations also become more detailed.
- **Each child's representations are unique.** Children express themselves in ways that make sense to them and reflect their interests, experiences, and personalities. They may be silly or

intense, slapdash or slow, indifferent or concerned about their audience. Adults should therefore view each child's artwork as a one-of-a-kind creation. Children, like adult artists, need emotional and physical space to create freely.
- **Young children are capable of appreciating as well as making art.** Educators may think art appreciation is too analytical for preschoolers. But because young children are so observant and use all their senses, they are ideal candidates for appreciating the world of art. In fact, they are often eager to share their reactions to a picture, song, or story. The key, says art educator Marjorie Schiller, is that "talking about art should spring from the interests of the children and be initiated, for the most part, by them" (1995, p. 34).

In the following small-group times, young children are engaged in both making and appreciating art. These activities stem from a wide range of children's interests; use diverse materials, tools, and techniques; and explore art in its many manifestations. For more information on early development in the arts and ideas for art activities, see *Supporting Young Artists: The Development of the Visual Arts in Young Children* (Epstein & Trimis, 2002) and *Round the Circle: Key Experiences in Movement for Young Children* (Weikart, 2000).

References

Arts Education Partnership. (1998). *Young children and the arts: Making creative connections — A report of the Task Force on Children's Learning and the Arts: Birth to age eight.* Washington, DC: Author.

Epstein, A. S., & Trimis, E. (2002). *Supporting young artists: The development of the visual arts in young children.* Ypsilanti, MI: HighScope Press.

Seefeldt, C. (1999). Art for young children. In C. Seefeldt (Ed.), *The early childhood curriculum: Current findings in theory and practice* (3rd ed.). New York: Teachers College Press, 201–217.

Weikart, P. S. (2000) *Round the circle: Key experiences in movement for young children* (2nd ed.). Ypsilanti, MI: HighScope Press.

36 Architecture All Around

Children build three-dimensional structures based on photographs of their neighborhood's architectural features, taken during the previous day's field trip.

Time of day: Small-Group Time

Content Area: The Arts: Visual Art

Materials

Materials for each child and teacher:

- Building materials (three-dimensional) such as unit blocks, Legos, modeling clay, or play dough

Shared materials:

- Photographs from the previous day's field trip around the local neighborhood to look at its architectural features, including buildings (e.g., apartments, houses, stores, office complexes); doorways (e.g., doors, awnings, stairs, railings); windows (e.g., with/without panes, trim, glass); brickwork (e.g., sidewalks, walls); and other characteristics.

Backup materials:

- Architectural magazines, books, and catalogs; real estate brochures; other architectural illustrations
- Photographs of the children's own homes (e.g., apartment buildings, houses) and familiar buildings outside the area of the walk (e.g., the local library, supermarket, movie theater, playground, mall); familiar storybooks that feature buildings and structures of different types
- Materials to decorate the structures (e.g., fabric scraps, pipe cleaners, squares of construction paper, beads, shells, pebbles)

Beginning

- Spread out the photographs and talk with children about the previous day's field trip, helping them to remember and describe the different architectural features they saw. Encourage children to hold, pass around, point to, and engage with the photographs.

- Choose one of the photographs and a three-dimensional building material (e.g., unit blocks) and say something like *I wonder if we can make a house that looks like the apartment building we saw on the corner.* (Together with the children, look at the photo of the building and point to and count the number of floors.) Wait to see if a child volunteers and shows how he or she would make the building. (If not, demonstrate.)
- Show the children the other building materials and say something like *I wonder what sorts of structures you can make.*

Middle

- Encourage children to look at the photographs as they explore the three-dimensional art materials. Talk with them about the features they see and might want to incorporate into their own building projects (e.g., size, proportions, colors, design features).
- Encourage children who are interested in working together to collaborate on projects.
- Take photographs of the structures the children make to use at recall time and in follow-up activities (see below).

End

- Together with the children, sort and put away the materials. Decide with the children where to put/post the photographs so they can refer to them at work/choice time.
- Ask the children to choose a way to move "like a tall or short building" to the next activity.

Ideas for follow-up

- In the art area, house area, and block area, post reproductions of artwork that highlight architectural features (e.g., cityscapes, rural scenes with barns and other outbuildings, tall monuments/sculptures, stone walls with engravings). In the book area, add books, magazines, and catalogs that focus on architectural features.

- Repeat the activity later in the year, providing children with materials (e.g., paper, crayons, markers, colored pencils) to create two-dimensional drawings.

- Make a display with the photos of the field trip and children's corresponding drawings and models. Share the display with parents. Encourage children and parents to compare photos of the real structures with the children's representations.

- Work with the children to make a book with pictures of their homes (apartment buildings, houses, etc.) and neighborhoods. (Ask parents to bring in photographs and/or take photos when you make home visits or travel to/from work.) Add the children's drawings to the book, with any related dictation or writing about the drawings they choose to include (e.g., what the drawings represent and/or how the children made them).

Adaptations for children with special needs

- For children with visual impairments, provide materials that focus on texture and allow for manipulation. Provide tools (e.g., textured rollers) that enable children to create and feel structural features. Make or provide models and encourage children to touch them and describe what they feel, emphasizing parts that poke out, have indentations/impressions, and/or showcase different textures.

- Encourage children with limited mobility to work on the floor (e.g., rolling, scooting) so their structures can extend beyond wheelchair trays or the table area in front of them. Help them — and encourage peers to help them — reach or use various materials they cannot access or manipulate on their own.

Developmental range: Supporting children at different levels

Earlier ⟶ **Middle** ⟶ **Later** ⟶

Earlier

Children may

- Explore the materials but not make representations of specific things (e.g., align or stack blocks; squeeze or roll play dough).
- Use the materials to represent something non-architectural (e.g., make molds of their family, an animal, an imaginary character).
- Talk about things they remember from the field trip; refer to architectural features (e.g., *We saw a bus; We walked right past my Aunt Sarah's house!*).
- Talk about the architectural features in the photos but not represent them with the materials (e.g., *I see a bench and another bench; What do you call that thing over the door?* [points to awning]).

Adults can

- Talk with children about what they are doing and making with the materials (e.g., *You're lining up the blocks; You made a big blue shape*).
- Comment on non-architectural representations, using descriptive and spatial language (e.g., *Your dog is tiny next to you*); suggest children look at a related book to see what other features they might include in their drawing/model.
- Build their own representation and describe its architectural features to children; listen/respond to children's observations (e.g., *I made windows upstairs and downstairs because my house is two stories; Yes, I remember from when I visited that your house is also two stories high*).

Middle

Children may

- Represent one architectural feature (one detail) (e.g., duplicate the height of a building with a corresponding number of unit blocks; use play dough the same color as a house).
- Describe one characteristic of their structure (e.g., put a small upright block on top of a large flat one and say, *This house has a chimney*; alternate colors of unit blocks and say, *These are the bricks — they go red, yellow, red, yellow*).
- Use simple spatial language to describe what they build (e.g., *There's a dog in front of the house; You gotta crawl under the fence; There's a flag pole next to the school*).

Adults can

- Show their own drawing or building to children, asking them to suggest additional details (e.g., *What else should I draw so it looks more like the pet store? What can I use to show the cracks in the wall of the garage?*).
- Comment on and encourage children to say more about the content or process of making their model; repeat and add to their words.
- Compare what children build to details in the photograph; encourage them to point out corresponding features (e.g., *Can you show me in the photo what this part on the bottom of your model is?*).
- Use and encourage children to use descriptive language related to color, shape, size, pattern, position, etc. (e.g., *Show me how you got this part to stand up straight; What colors will you use for the bricks?*).

Later

Children may

- Represent two or more architectural features (at least two details) (e.g., mold a rectangle shape out of play dough and press on fabric squares for curtains).
- Describe two or more characteristics of their structure (e.g., *That's the garage door; it's red and it looks like waffle pretzels*).
- Compare architectural features in a photo to those in their own representations (e.g., point to photo and model and say, *See, there's blue curtains in all the windows and I used the blue marker on mine too*).
- Add architectural features that are not in the photograph to their own representation (e.g., *That's called a door knocker and my mommy nailed one on our house*).

Adults can

- Comment on the details in the child's model; repeat and add to the child's use of descriptive words (e.g., *The black-and-white stripes make a pattern just like the zebra in the zoo book!*).
- Encourage children to add and describe details; ask them where/how they will use the materials (e.g., *How will you attach the clay after you roll it into a coil?*).
- Show their own representations to children and ask them to suggest details that are not in the photograph (e.g., *Suppose the family that lived there decided to make their house bigger. How could I build that?*).
- Ask children how other structures they are familiar with are the same as or different from those in the photos and models.

37 Blueprints

Children build structures from wood scraps based on plans they have drawn.

Time of day: Small-Group Time

Content Area: The Arts: Visual Art

Materials

Materials for each child and teacher:

- Wood scraps of different sizes (large/small; long/short; thick/thin) and shapes (e.g., square, rectangle, triangle, irregular)

- Blue paper and pencils

- Large pieces of cardboard and/or newspaper (to use as a base and make it easier for children to carry their structures to a drying location; also helpful in protecting tabletop from glue spills)

- Glue bottles (or cups for glue) and small paintbrushes

Shared materials:

- Blueprints or other architectural drawings and building plans (available online or at your local library); pictures of wooden structures (e.g., drawings and photographs from architecture/design magazines); and/or miniature replicas of structures made out of wood (e.g., barns, log cabins, birdhouses, bridges, and ships available through craft catalogues and at hobby supply shops, etc.)

Backup materials:

- Other scrap pieces (e.g., corks, tongue depressors, Popsicle sticks, bark, plastic lids, caps from milk cartons)

Beginning

- Spread building plans out on table and ask children, *What do you think these are?* Wait for children to respond. Say, *These are called blueprints (or building plans), and architects use these to make a plan for how they will build something like a house or garage or bridge.* Share some pictures of wooden structures.

- Pass out a set of materials to each child and say, *You can use these materials to construct something out of wood, too. If you build your structure*

on the cardboard (or newspaper), you can move it more easily later. There is blue paper and a pencil, if you want to draw your plan first.*

Middle

- Encourage children to first think about what they want to make, and suggest they draw it so they can refer to their plans when they are putting the structure together (e.g., *To help you remember what you want to do, you can first draw your plan. Then you can look at the plan as you build with your wood. This is what architects do when they make the kinds of drawings we were looking at.*)

- Comment on and acknowledge what children are doing (e.g., *It looks like you are trying to get this piece to stand up. I wonder how you'll do that; You stacked these together and glued them in the middle; You're constructing something that is really tall*).

- Problem-solve with children about how they are going to put their wood structures together. Refer children to one another for assistance, and offer your assistance when needed.

- Some children prefer not to talk when they are concentrating on an activity such as building. Respect their desire for silence. Sit next to them and observe and/or imitate what they are doing. Wait for children to initiate conversation; if they don't, continue to provide silent support.

End

- Let children know that if they don't finish their project today they can put a "work-in-progress" sign on their construction and put it in a safe place until work/choice time the following day.

- Have children place extra materials and glue back in their baskets or in one place on the table.

- Suggest that children pretend their arms and hands are glued to their bodies as they move to the next activity.

Ideas for follow-up
- Place materials in the woodworking area for children to use at work time.
- Ask children who plan to work in the block area or construction area at work/choice time if they want to draw a blueprint of what they will make. At recall time, encourage children to draw what they made.
- At work/choice or recall times, ask children who drew their plans to compare their drawings to their finished constructions to see how they are the same or different.

- Plan another small-group time for children to paint their constructions.
- Bring wood scraps outside for children to use in the sandbox or dirt.

Adaptations for children with special needs
- Encourage children with visual limitations to explore small-scale wooden models with their hands.
- Provide plastic gloves and smocks/shirts for children uncomfortable working with glue.

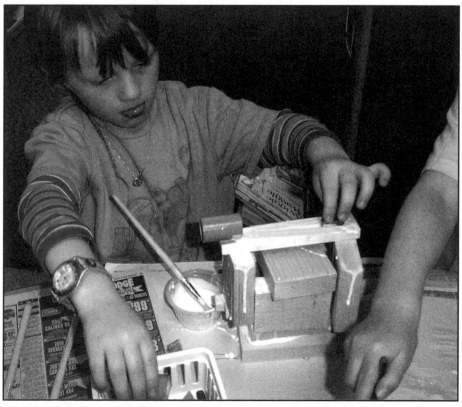

Children in the earlier developmental range may glue wood together without a plan in mind. Others, in a later stage of development, may draw a plan and follow it while building.

Developmental range: Supporting children at different levels

Earlier ⟶

Children may
- Explore the wood and/or glue in simple ways (e.g., stack, line up, or rearrange wood; watch the glue run over a piece of wood; place scrap items on top of wood and squeeze glue over everything).
- Glue wood together without a specific plan in mind; describe what they did (e.g., *I put the big block on top and the small one here*).
- Make a structure and then decide it looks like something (e.g., *Hey, this looks like a sandwich*).

Adults can
- Use materials, following children's lead.
- Acknowledge what children are doing by repeating and restating their words (e.g., *Oh, you are making a fast car*).
- Make a structure and ask children what they think it might represent.

Middle ⟶

Children may
- Draw a simple plan for what they will make using one or two details (e.g., draw a rectangle and say it is a plan for a doghouse); follow through with plan or not.
- Intentionally place wood and/or apply glue where they want it.
- Describe what they are doing and what they made in simple terms (e.g., *I made a birdhouse so the birds can have a place to live*).

Adults can
- Describe children's actions (e.g., *You are pressing with two hands to make sure the wood sticks together*).
- Talk with children about their plan, and bring their attention back to it after they've completed their structure (e.g., *I see from your plan you had a piece of wood here. Did you change your mind? Let's take a look at your plan now that you are done constructing and compare the two*).
- Talk with children about the process they are using to put their structures together.

Later ⟶

Children may
- Draw a complex plan about what they will make with three or more details (e.g., draw a square with vertical lines and a door and say it is an alligator cage); refer to their plan while building and compare their plan to the finished product.
- Describe what they are doing and making in detail (e.g., *This is a corral for horses. Here's the fence and the gate, and these four pieces of wood make a holder for the hay*).
- Use materials in more advanced ways and with greater skill (e.g., get vise to hold two pieces of wood together; balance pieces of wood to get them to stay together).

Adults can
- Allow children to problem-solve with materials and assist when needed by asking open-ended questions, (e.g., *If you wanted something for tires, I wonder what you could use*). If a child cannot come up with a solution, offer a suggestion (e.g., *You could use the round plastic lids or cardboard scraps*).
- Refer children to one another for ideas about their structures (e.g., *Chesney put her triangular piece of wood under the tall piece and it stayed together. You could ask her how she did that*).
- Acknowledge and describe the complex ways children are using tools and materials.

38 Drawing With Oil Pastels

Children use oil pastels to draw pictures and talk with the teacher and one another about the process and experience.

Time of day: Small-Group Time   **Content Area:** The Arts: Visual Art

Materials

Materials for each child and teacher:
- 1 piece of white drawing paper
- 1 oil pastel crayon (if possible, give each child the same color to begin with, or use a limited number of colors and encourage children to switch or trade if they choose)

Shared materials:
- None

Backup materials:
- Other oil pastel colors
- Extra paper
- Regular wax crayons

Beginning

- Tell the children a story about a young child who draws pictures. For example, you might say the following: *Once a little girl got a special kind of crayon called an oil pastel. She took it with her on a walk, along with some paper. Sometimes she just made marks on the paper to see what the oil pastel felt like and how it looked on the paper. Other times she drew pictures of things she saw on her walk.*
- Give each child a set of materials and say something like *I wonder how you will use your oil pastel to draw on your paper.*

Middle

- Imitate children's actions by using the oil pastels, but keep your drawing abstract (e.g., scribble; make marks, lines, and polka dots; outline or fill in shapes) so children will be less likely to ask you to draw specific representations for them.
- Comment on and encourage children to talk about what they are drawing and how it feels to draw with the oil pastel. You might say, *Tell me about what you are drawing; I wonder what you drew over on this side of your paper;* or *How does it feel when you are moving the oil pastel across your paper?* Repeat and rephrase children's words, and add new vocabulary to what they have said, such as *It feels* smooth *to you when you draw with the oil pastel* or *The pastel feels* slippery *when you draw on your paper — it glides across the page.*
- Midway through the activity, give children regular wax crayons and encourage them to compare the crayons to the oil pastels. Talk with them about how and why the two media are different.

End

- Tell children the oil pastels will be available in the art area if they want to use them again.
- Have children put their pictures in their cubbies to take home, or ask them if they want to hang them on the wall. Offer assistance if needed. If children want to continue working on the same picture, store it in a safe place with a work-in-progress sign.
- Have children slide to the next activity "like an oil pastel sliding across the paper."

Ideas for follow-up

- Add the book *Harold and the Purple Crayon* to the book area. Read the book and have children compare their experiences and any stories they make up about their drawings to Harold's.
- Bring in art books showing line drawings and designs from various artists so children can look through them during book time or work/choice time in the art area.
- Introduce children to other types of media for drawing, such as colored pencils, silky crayons, chalk, and water crayons.
- Draw with water and paintbrushes on pavement at outside time.

Adaptations for children with special needs

- Use wide pastels or silky crayons (similar to oil pastels but thicker).
- Tape down paper on the table so it will not move around while the child is drawing.
- Use writing splints to hold the oil pastels so children can manipulate them more easily.
- Provide extra lighting (e.g., lamps, natural light) for children with visual limitations.

As a follow-up to drawing with oil pastels, introduce children to other drawing media such as colored pencils, silky crayons, chalk, and water crayons.

Developmental range: Supporting children at different levels

Earlier →

Children may
- Scribble on the paper or draw big loops and circles.
- Make distinct marks and lines on the paper.
- Draw something on the paper and then say what it looks like (e.g., *Look. I made a hat!*).
- Ask for help in drawing an object.
- Identify colors (correctly or incorrectly).

Adults can
- Imitate children's actions (e.g., draw big circles, copy the kinds of marks and lines they make).
- Comment on what children are doing (e.g., *You are using the red pastel and making small marks on your paper*).
- Problem-solve with children who ask for help with their drawing (e.g., *I wonder how you can make a bike; How does a bike look? Let's see if we have a bike in one of our books you can look at*); refer children to one another for help (e.g., ask other children if they know how to draw a bike and if they can assist the child who asked for help).
- Use color names correctly but do not correct children if they use them incorrectly.

Middle →

Children may
- Use the oil pastel in different ways (e.g., draw or dab with the point, roll it or rub it up and down on the paper).
- Draw something with intention; make something and say what it represents (e.g., *This is going to be a spaceship*).
- Draw a picture that includes one or two details (e.g., draw a square topped by a triangle and call it a *house*).
- Talk about what or how they draw with the pastels (e.g., *I drew stripes; You can use the tip to make lots of spots*).
- Correctly name the colors in their picture (e.g., *I have a purple pastel. And then I used the yellow crayon for the sun*).

Adults can
- Comment on the different ways children are using the pastels and describe their actions (e.g., *You're pressing really hard on your paper with the pastel. Look what you made when you pressed really hard. It's dark*).
- Repeat and/or restate what children are saying about their pictures (e.g., *You made a red boat. I wonder what else you will make; Your house has two shapes — a square and a triangle on top of it*).
- Bring children's attention to designs and colors in their pictures (e.g., *How did you get these vertical lines so wide?; When you keep coloring over the same spot, the pastel gets thicker. Feel this spot and now feel this spot. Do they feel the same?*).

Later →

Children may
- Describe the experience of using the oil pastel (e.g., *It feels slippery; This is smooth; It leaves color on my fingers; You can fill in all the spaces really easy*).
- Draw a picture (a recognizable object or person) that includes three or more details (e.g., *It's my dad's garden. Here's the tomatoes and beans and peppers. And this is the fence to keep out rabbits*).
- Make up their own stories about what they are drawing; point to different parts of their picture while telling the story.
- Compare the oil pastel and crayon; say how/why they are the same or different (e.g., *This goes faster on the page; It's the same color but maybe darker; I think the oil makes it slippery*).

Adults can
- Acknowledge, support, and extend children's observations about the art medium (e.g., *My pastel left smudges on my fingers too; It's so smooth it is easy to fill in all the white spaces!*).
- Talk with children about the details in their drawings (e.g., *Rabbits get into my garden too. Does the fence keep them out?*).
- Write down children's dictated stories about their drawings and read them back.
- Encourage children to describe and compare the pastel and the crayon; support and extend their comments (e.g., *Can you show me how one goes faster than the other?; Why do you think the oil pastel purple is darker than the crayon purple?*).

39 Embossing With Tinfoil

Children explore the technique of embossing by rubbing tinfoil over objects to create designs and patterns.

Time of day: Small-Group Time   **Content Area:** The Arts: Visual Art

Materials

Materials for each child and teacher:

- 2–3 large pieces of tinfoil, approximately one-foot square
- Several thick paper towels
- Tool to rub with (e.g., chopstick, Popsicle stick, pen with cap, pencil eraser, large pencil, crayon)
- Items to emboss (e.g., shells, leaves, bark, carpet, coins, chains, buttons, ribbon, screen, combs, stencils, rubber bands, paper clips, pumice, sponges, sequins, netting)

Shared materials:

- None

Backup materials:

- Extra pieces of tinfoil

Beginning

- Place a coin on top of a paper towel with a piece of foil over it and say to the children *What do you think will happen to the coin under the foil if I gently rub on top of the foil with the chopstick?* After children respond, gently rub on top of and around the coin. As the coin's image surfaces on the foil, ask the children *What do you see when I gently rub on the foil where it covers the coin?* Tell the children *This is called embossing. You make an imprint of the coin in the foil.*
- Pass out materials to each child and say *Here are some items for you to rub and tools to rub with so you can make your own embossed picture on the foil.*

Middle

- Remind children to be gentle as they rub their foil, pointing out that if they rub too hard, the pressure may make a hole in the foil. Problem-solve with children if they do make a hole in their foil and then get upset. Ask them for ideas about what they would like to do to solve the problem, or prompt them for suggestions (e.g., *Would you like to fix it? How would you like to do this?; Would you like another piece of foil?*).
- Converse with children about what they are doing and what is happening to the foil. Repeat children's words and add new words to describe their actions, the results, and the art techniques involved (e.g., rubbing, pressing, outlining; making patterns, imprints, or impressions).
- Refer children to one another for assistance, and encourage them to observe and compare the designs they are making (e.g., *Look at the ridges you made when you were rubbing the shell. Myra made the same ridges on her foil; I wonder what you used to get this design because Luis has the same design on his foil. I wonder if you used the same item*).

End

- Have children sort and put away their items. Ask them if they want to put their foil pictures in their cubbies or post them on the wall.
- Remind children where the materials are stored should they want to use them during work/choice time.
- Have children glide their feet across the floor (the way they gently glided their chopsticks across the foil) as they move to the next part of the day.

Ideas for follow-up

- Bring in art books and reproductions, stationery, and other items with embossing.
- Take foil and rubbing tools outside so children can emboss items such as bark, gravel, flowers, and brickwork on the side of buildings.

Adaptations for children with special needs

- Encourage children with visual limitations to feel the texture of the objects and the impressions they make through the foil.

Developmental range: Supporting children at different levels

Earlier ⟶

Children may

- Play with the objects, foil, or tools (e.g., roll coins, crinkle or tear the foil).
- Use tools or objects to make simple marks on or holes in the foil (e.g., poke a hole, press or push items onto foil).
- Say what their marks look like (e.g., *I made a hole for the snakes to live in; Look, I made a sun*).
- Rub a tool over the foil but not put an object underneath; express surprise or disappointment when no embossed image appears.

Adults can

- Imitate the actions of children (e.g., *I'm rolling my foil in a ball too; I wonder if I can stack my leaves as tall as yours*).
- Describe what children are doing (e.g., *I see your object is poking through the tinfoil; You are moving the shell back and forth on the tinfoil*).
- Encourage children to use various objects to make imprints (e.g., *I wonder what impression a shell would make if you rubbed it in the tinfoil?; Let's try the comb to see what will happen*).
- Say *I wonder why you didn't get an imprint. What do you think you could do differently?*

Middle ⟶

Children may

- Choose an object to emboss and explain why (e.g., *I'm using the bark. I want to see if I can make bumps*).
- Concentrate on rubbing the objects; problem-solve if foil tears (e.g., *I rubbed too hard. [Get another piece of foil.] There, that's better*).
- Describe one or two details of the embossing process or the imprint they made (e.g., *Look what I did. It's bumpy; I used my finger to rub the screen*).

Adults can

- Comment on and encourage children to talk about their choice of objects (e.g., *What made you choose the button next?; You did a whole row of shells*).
- Acknowledge children's problem-solving efforts (e.g., *You rubbed softer, and this time the foil didn't tear*).
- Refer children to one another's imprints (e.g., *Darian's embossing looks the same as yours. I wonder what he used; Cammie pushed gently on the foil with the shell underneath. See if that works for you*).
- Try children's ideas and compare (e.g., *Yours made long ridges but mine are short; I used a sponge too. I wonder why they look different*).

Later ⟶

Children may

- Predict what an imprint will look like based on the object's attributes (e.g., *It'll be round, 'cause the coin is round; My embossing will have stripes like the comb*).
- Try different ways and tools to emboss the objects (e.g., use chopsticks and then rub shell with their fingers).
- Describe three or more details of the process or imprint (e.g., *I rubbed hard with the pencil and you can see the circle and middle of the penny*).
- Describe and compare the imprints made by different objects (e.g., *The shell made lines on top but not the button*).

Adults can

- Ask children to describe their process and imitate it (e.g., *How could I make an embossing that looks just like yours?*).
- Encourage children to predict what an imprint will look like by examining the object (e.g., *I wonder what design the sequins will make*).
- Add vocabulary to children's conversations (e.g., *Gena made sharp ridges; Look at the pattern Jerzy made with the pumice*).
- Discuss the different imprints and the tools and objects used to emboss them (e.g., *Which object did you use to get this imprint? How did you rub it?; How did you make this design?*).

40 Favorite Illustrations and Collage Materials

Children look at a familiar picture book with photocollage illustrations, then create their own collages using materials based on those used in the book.

Time of day: Small-Group Time | **Content Area:** The Arts: Visual Art

Materials

Materials for each child and teacher:

- Paper circles or paper plates, at least 10" in diameter
- Birdseed, kernels of field corn, yarn or string, shells, buttons, bottlecaps

Shared materials:

- The book *Snowballs* by Lois Ehlert

Backup materials:

- Glue and extra supply of the materials

Beginning

- Show the children the book *Snowballs* and talk briefly about what they remember from having read it before. Lay the book on the table or floor and invite the children to look at the photocollage illustrations with you.
- Ask them to talk about what they see in the pictures, and listen to their ideas.
- Tell the children that they are going to create their own illustrations using some of these same materials the artist used in creating her book.

Middle

- Move from child to child and watch and comment on how they use the materials. Talk with them about the properties of the materials, how they combine them, and what their collages look like (color, shape, size, texture, etc.).
- Expect that children will use the materials in a variety of ways.
- Give each child a bottle of glue.

End

- As children are cleaning up, remind them where they can find the materials at work/choice time.
- Transition children to the next part of the daily routine according to the materials they used in their collage. Say something like *If you used red yarn, you can go wash your hands for snack;* or *If you used bottle tops, you can go wash your hands.*

Ideas for follow-up

- Try the same idea with other familiar books and art materials (e.g., make colored-paper collages after looking at the picture book *Brown Bear, Brown Bear, What Do You See?* by Bill Martin and Eric Carle; or use watercolors and very runny tempera paint along with the book *Old Black Fly* by Jim Aylesworth and Stephen Gammell).
- After you have read a book many times, draw children's attention to the illustrations. Together with children, discuss how the artist might have created them. Invite children to try those materials in the art area.

Adaptations for children with special needs

- Use adaptive devices, such as easy-to-grip scissors, so the child can manipulate the materials.
- Offer large and bright materials for children with visual limitations.

Developmental range: Supporting children at different levels

Earlier →

Children may
- Make glue puddles on their page.
- Glue one object on top of another.
- Glue objects to the paper.
- Comment on the process or physical properties of the materials (e.g., *The glue is runny; These things* [pine cones] *are prickly*).
- Use as many materials as they can.

Adults can
- Comment on what you see children doing (e.g., *Jemal, you are squeezing lots of glue along the top of your page*).
- Imitate the children's actions.
- Invite the children to use some of the backup materials.

Middle →

Children may
- Use the materials to create simple representations with one or two features.
- Name the parts of their picture (e.g., *These are the eyes, and this is the hair*).
- Line up the materials and glue them in a pattern.

Adults can
- Comment on the properties of the materials (e.g., *The yarn is long and wavy*).
- Notice other parts of children's work (e.g., *You've got buttons along the bottom*). Listen to any comments that the child might add.
- Offer to write down the child's description on a sticky note and display it near their work.
- Acknowledge the patterns children create with materials (e.g., *You made a pattern with the beads. It goes red, blue; red, blue; red, blue*).

Later →

Children may
- Use the materials to create detailed representations with three or more features.
- Share stories about what they made (e.g., *This is the baby snowman. He's crying because his mommy is far away*).
- Say why they chose certain materials to represent specific features (e.g., *I made the eyes with sequins 'cause they're shiny*).
- Ask to use other materials from the art area to better fit the ideas they have in mind (e.g., *Miss Penny, can I get the scissors to cut this smaller? I need some yarn to use for hair*).

Adults can
- Comment on the details of children's work (e.g., *There are five little pieces on the end of this circle*). Listen to any comments the child might add.
- Offer to write down the children's stories on a sticky note and display it near their work.
- Comment on the shared properties of the material and the feature(s) the child is representing.
- Encourage children to add to their work using additional materials from the art area.

Young children learn to appreciate art by exploring different artistic techniques. Here a young boy creates a collage after looking at and discussing the illustrations in Lois Ehlert's book Snowballs.

41 Making Marks in Dough

Children make marks in play dough, creating and exploring different designs and patterns.

Time of day: Small-Group Time

Content Area: The Arts: Visual Art

Materials

Materials for each child and teacher:
- A ball of play dough
- Collection of several pebbles and twigs
- Small basket or container

Shared materials:
- None

Backup materials:
- Shells (with smooth and textured surfaces)

Beginning
- Give each child a ball of play dough. Talk to them about the marks they can make in the play dough with their fingers. Tell them that for small-group time, they will also have other objects to work with, which will make different kinds of marks in their dough.
- Give each child a small container with the pebbles and twigs.
- Invite children to explore the different kinds of marks that these objects make in the dough.

Middle
- Move from child to child, observing and commenting on how children are using the materials and imitating what they do.
- When commenting on children's work, use vocabulary related to the graphic elements of their designs (e.g., using words such as *lines, circles, patterns, textures*).
- Add the shells to the middle of the table to extend children's experiences.

End
- Ask children to sort pebbles, twigs, and shells into three large containers. Remind them where these materials are kept in the classroom in case they want to make plans to use them for work/choice time.
- Suggest that children make their bodies look like either a twig or a pebble as they move to the next part of the daily routine.

Ideas for follow-up
- After a few weeks, repeat the activity using other materials that will make interesting imprints in the dough (e.g., small Legos, pine cones, treaded tires from small-wheeled toys, kitchen flatware and cooking utensils, carpentry hardware and tools).
- Notice and point out the graphic elements of other things in your environment (e.g., patterns on fabric, designs made by the sun and shadows on the carpet, brick patterns in the hallway, tire treads in the mud, bare/empty surfaces versus those that are filled/crowded).

Adaptations for children with special needs
- Be sure to provide objects that are easy to grip and hold.
- Include items that leave large, easy-to-see marks in the dough.

Developmental range: Supporting children at different levels

Earlier

Children may
- Squeeze and poke the dough.
- "Hide" (bury) all their pebbles in the dough.
- Use the dough to make simple "balls" or "snakes."

Adults can
- Imitate what the child is doing.
- Notice the holes that the child's finger makes in the dough. Wonder aloud if there is anything else in the child's basket that might make holes.
- Hide another material in the dough and see if the child can guess what it is (e.g., a shell or a small twig).
- Follow the child's lead in exploring and using the dough (e.g., if the child makes a snake, the adult can make one too and playfully have it "talk" to the child's snake).

Middle

Children may
- Make a ball with their dough and cover it with pebbles.
- Stick a twig in a hunk of dough and call it a *tree*.
- Use their materials to make imprints in the dough.

Adults can
- Take a pebble out of the dough and draw the child's attention to the mark it made.
- Make comments on the marks (the effects) the materials leave in the dough (e.g., *When you drag the twig across the dough, it makes squiggly lines. When you poked it in the dough, it made holes*).
- Make a mark in their own dough and ask children if they can guess how the imprint was made.

Later

Children may
- Create patterns with their materials or with the marks they make in their dough.
- Use a twig to draw on their dough.
- Request additional materials to complete their design (e.g., *Hey Polly, I need some more pebbles to finish this side*).

Adults can
- Make simple patterns with the marks in their dough and ask children if they would like to extend the pattern.
- Make comments on the graphic elements of children's designs and patterns, using words like *straight, circular, dotted, angular, close together, far apart, empty space, filled space, even, uneven, smooth,* and *rough*.
- Wonder aloud what it would look like to use two materials together to mark the dough; ask the child to predict what the mark might look like.

42 Molding and Sculpting With Clay

Children look at pictures of objects made of clay, then create their own sculptures using a ball of clay and a variety of sculpting tools.

Time of day: Small-Group Time

Content Area: The Arts: Visual Art

Materials

Materials for each child and teacher:

- Ball of clay in a container (cover clay with a damp paper towel to keep it moist until small-group time)
- Sculpting and carving tools for working with clay, and items from classroom interest areas (e.g., plastic knives, forks, chopsticks, spoons, forks, rolling pin, garlic press, pieces of wood, combs, picks, hammers, screwdrivers, nails, golf tees)
- Base for children to work on and use to move sculptures to a place for drying (e.g., sturdy cardboard, plastic tray, wooden slab)

Shared materials:

- Postcards, pictures, or photos (e.g., from magazines) of sculptures or items made with clay (e.g., statues, ceramics)
- Objects made of clay, such as pottery vases, bowls, mugs, tiles, plates (optional)
- Chart paper and markers (to record children's predictions about what will happen to the clay when it dries)

Backup materials:

- Additional rolling pins

Beginning

- Say *Today I brought in some pictures of sculptures that artists made from clay,* and encourage children to examine and talk about pictures of items made of clay and/or actual clay objects. If you've brought in clay objects for children to look at you might add, *I also brought in some pottery — things like bowls, vases, and plates — that are also made from clay.*

- Explain how artists work with clay by saying something like *Artists shape the clay with their hands. They also use different tools to help them shape and decorate their sculptures.*

- Distribute the materials and say *You can be an artist and sculpt whatever you would like with your clay. You can use your hands and also these other tools to help you sculpt. If you work on these bases, we can move your sculptures to a safe place to dry when you're done.*

Seeing the artwork of others, such as clay pots and pictures of ceramics, can inspire children as they explore materials and use tools to mold and sculpt their own creations.

Middle

- Imitate and comment on what you see children doing with the clay.
- Encourage children to use the clay in different ways. Talk to them about their actions, repeating the words they use and introducing new vocabulary (e.g., *push, pull, roll, pound, stack, scrap, score, cut, poke, squeeze, mold, sculpt, pinch, coil, press, flatten, stamp*).
- Talk with children about the characteristics of the clay, using words such as *density, thickness, weight, temperature, texture,* and *hue/color.* Use adjectives such as *light/heavy, cold/warm, soft/hard,* and other descriptive words. Also, talk with them about how the clay changes when they mold it in different ways (e.g., Ask *What happened to the clay when you twisted it around?* or *I wonder what the piece of clay will look like when you coil it into a long piece*).
- Pose the question, *What do you think will happen to your sculpture when it dries?* Record children's predictions on chart paper. (See Ideas for follow-up.)
- Respect children's desire for silence. Some children prefer not to talk when they are concentrating on building or making something. Sit next to them and observe and/or imitate what they are doing. Wait to see if a child initiates a conversation; if not, continue to provide silent support.
- Do not assume that something a child has made represents a particular object or person. Children may or may not represent objects with their sculptures. Follow the child's lead before referring to something by name. Do not "name" an object unless the child does.

End

- Have children put away the tools and unused clay and move their sculptures to a safe place to dry. Children who want to continue working on their pieces can put a work-in-progress sign next to their project.
- Ask children to pretend their bodies are made of heavy clay as they move to the next activity.

Ideas for follow-up

- Follow up the next day(s) to observe the changes that occur in the clay during the drying process (e.g., note drying time, color changes, shrinkage). Refer back to children's predictions (see middle of activity), and compare these to what actually happened.
- Take pictures of children's sculptures and have them available during the next clay activity so that children can compare the similarities and differences between their two projects.
- After children have had time to explore with the clay, conduct another small-group time during which you give children small cups of water and/or wet sponges that they can add/apply to the clay. Talk about what happens to the clay when water is added to it.
- Bring in pictures of sculptures and other three-dimensional models made by artists that children can look at and use as a model for their own projects. Invite families to bring in artwork made of ceramics.
- For future exploration with clay, use toothpicks, marbles, cookie cutters, and textured materials (e.g., shells, stamps, buttons, coins, rocks, pumice) to make imprints.
- Arrange to visit the studio of a local sculptor and/or a ceramic artist who works in clay or similar materials.

Adaptations for children with special needs

- Encourage children to stand instead of sitting for this activity so they can use all their body strength to manipulate and mold the clay.
- Give children small and medium-sized balls of clay for easy and harder manipulation.

Developmental range: Supporting children at different levels

Earlier →

Children may

- Manipulate clay with simple actions (e.g., pound, cut, poke, roll, drop, pull apart).
- Manipulate the clay, then say what they think the clay looks like (e.g., snake, pizza, cookies, ball, pancake).
- Explore the clay using one or two tools (e.g., poke or press something into the clay and examine the hole or impression it leaves).
- Repeat the same action over and over.

Adults can

- Imitate children's actions.
- Describe their own sculpture (e.g., *I made a snake; Mine is a bowl*).
- Describe children's actions (e.g., *You are pounding really hard on your clay; I see Henry poking his clay with the wooden tool*).
- Ask open-ended questions sparingly (e.g., *I wonder what will happen if you scrape the clay with your fingernails or with your fork; How did you make this design here on your clay?*).
- Follow children's lead (e.g., if children pretend they made cupcakes and offer one, the adult can play along).

Middle →

Children may

- Make something with intention (e.g., tear off pieces of clay and roll them into small balls for "blueberries"; announce they are going to make pancakes and roll out several circles).
- Explore and compare the effect of using various tools (e.g., flatten clay and make cutting marks with knife; make large holes with chopsticks and small holes with fork tines).
- Sculpt figure with one or two details and name the object (e.g., make a flat circle with a ball on top and say, *It's a plate with a meatball*).

Adults can

- Ask children to describe how they did something (e.g., *How did you get your blueberries so small?*), and imitate the process.
- Repeat and restate children's words (e.g., *That's the tunnel that the cars go through; Show me again the poison you put in the cookies for the monsters to eat*).
- Draw children's attention to the effects of their use of different techniques and tools (e.g., *These holes look different from those. What did you use/do that made these wide and these narrow?*).
- Review with children what they made and how they made it (e.g., *Tell me about what you made out of your clay; I wonder how you got this part of the clay so smooth*).

Later →

Children may

- State a plan for what they want to make (e.g., *I'm going to make a dog and roll a long tail for it*) and carry out their idea.
- Sculpt figures with three or more details (e.g., mold clay figure with eyes, nose, mouth, hair, hands, and feet).
- Manipulate clay with more advanced skills (e.g., make pinch pot or bowl; tear off and shape smaller and/or thinner pieces; carve or press designs into surface).

Adults can

- Discuss children's plans, the materials they will need, and the steps they will take to carry them out. When children are done, ask if they followed their plans or changed them (and if so, why and how).
- Encourage children to describe in detail what they are making and how; refer to objects using the children's own labels for them (e.g., *I wonder what body parts you will make for your person; I wonder how you will make hair for your dog*).
- Encourage children to look at photos, pictures, and drawings for ideas on what to make and how to add detail or design to their sculptures.

43 Molding With Shaving Cream and Glue

Children mix together shaving cream and glue on heavy paper, creating designs and shapes that harden.

Time of day: Small-Group Time

Content Area: The Arts: Visual Art

Materials

Materials for each child and teacher:
- A bowl of shaving cream
- Small paper cup containing liquid glue
- Cardstock or thick paper
- Spoons
- Smock

Shared materials:
- None

Backup materials:
- Colored foil, confetti, or sequins/spangles

Beginning
- Introduce the activity by saying something like *Today we have two types of art materials that we are going to mix together: shaving cream and glue.*
- Give each child a set of materials. Make a comment such as *Let's see what happens when you mix together shaving cream and glue. I wonder what you will notice.*

Middle
- Imitate children's actions with your own materials.
- Comment on and describe children's actions and effects. Repeat their words and add new vocabulary words (e.g., *You are* molding *your glue into the shaving cream with both hands; I see you are* stirring *yours together with the spoon; It's forming* stiff peaks).
- Ask open-ended questions, such as *I wonder how it feels; What is happening to the shaving cream when you stir in the glue?; What do you think will happen when it dries?; What kinds of designs can you make with your fingers?*
- Introduce bits of colored foil, confetti, or sequins for children to add to their mixtures.

End
- Put all the creations in the middle of the table and encourage children to talk about and compare them. Repeat their words and add new vocabulary (see examples in the middle of activity) to describe and compare what they did, what they felt and saw happening, and what they made.
- Remind children where they can find these materials if they want to continue exploring and creating with them at work/choice time.
- Make up rhymes using children's names to support their transition to the next part of the day (e.g., *This shaving cream looks like a* hen, *said Ben. Ben can go to large group; This shaving cream is* smelly, *said Ellie*). You can also use made-up words to create a rhyme (e.g., *This shaving cream feels* dacob, *said Jacob*). Encourage children to make up rhymes with their own names.

Ideas for follow-up
- As the shaving cream is drying, or after it has dried, talk with the children about what they think happened to it. (Shaving cream will get puffy.)
- Mix shaving cream and food coloring.

Adaptations for children with special needs

- Provide plastic gloves for children who are sensitive to sensory experiences or concerned about getting their hands dirty.

- Encourage children with visual limitations to feel the mixture as they add more glue and as the mixture dries. Suggest they might want to use sparkly materials for easy-to-see effects.

Developmental range: Supporting children at different levels

Earlier ⟶

Children may
- Explore shaving cream and/or glue in simple ways (e.g., squeeze, fold, pat, mix with fingers, push across cardstock).
- Describe in simple language what the material feels like and what they are doing and/or making (e.g., *I'm making pie. This feels yucky*).

Adults can
- Imitate children's actions using the same materials.
- Describe their own actions and what they are making (e.g., *I'm twirling my shaving cream and glue together with my finger. I wonder how you will mix yours; I'm folding the shaving cream*).
- Talk about how the shaving cream and glue makes their hands feel. Repeat their words and add new words such as *messy, gooey, sticky, crusty, stiff.*

Middle ⟶

Children may
- Explore shaving cream and/or glue in two or more ways (e.g., mix and then spread it on the paper; use the spoon to stir the mixture and make mounds).
- Make/mold something with one or two details (e.g., *Here's the mountain and this is the ski trail*).
- Talk in more detail about what they are seeing, feeling, doing, and making (e.g., *It's getting thicker; These are swirly and these are smooth*).

Adults can
- Encourage children to describe their actions and the effects they observe. Repeat their words and add new ones (e.g., *You're stirring and spreading; Some people call those mounds. They look like little mountains*).
- Ask open-ended questions about what children are doing and making with the shaving cream and glue (e.g., *How did you make it hold together in such a big pile?; How did the bear get inside the tent?*).
- Refer children to one another for ideas on how to work with the materials.

Later ⟶

Children may
- Describe in detail their actions and the effects these create (e.g., *When you spread it all the way to the edge, it gets thinner. You can see the paper through it*).
- Make/mold something with three or more details (e.g., *It's my Grannie. See her eyes and nose and mouth, and that's all her curly white hair*).
- Create a story about what they are making (e.g., *They went to the beach and this is the sand. There are shells buried underneath and they dug for them with the spoon*).

Adults can
- Ask children if the shaving cream and glue and/or the things they make with these materials feel or look like something familiar (e.g., *Do those swirly white piles remind you of anything?*).
- Talk with children about changes that occur as shaving cream dries. Bring children's attention to areas that are already drying.
- Talk with children about their creations and encourage them to create stories about them; make comments and ask open-ended, follow-up questions to encourage children to elaborate on their ideas.

44 Outside Collage

Children collaborate on making a collage, using materials collected on a walk outdoors the previous day.

Time of day: Small-Group Time   **Content Area:** The Arts: Visual Art

Materials

Materials for each child and teacher:

- Sorted objects children collected outside the previous day (e.g., leaves, twigs, pebbles, shells, blades of grass, seed pods, acorns, pine cones)
- Glue sticks and small squeeze-bottles of glue

Shared materials:

- A long sheet of roll paper in an open area, such as the floor or play yard; set this out before small-group time begins

Backup materials:

- Other collage materials (e.g., small pieces of colored paper, yarn and ribbons, plastic bottle caps, scraps of wood)
- Individual pieces of paper (if children prefer to make their own collages)

Beginning

- Talk with the children about their experiences collecting objects on the previous day's walk (e.g., where they went, what they saw, what they collected). Let them know that today they will glue the objects they collected to make a "collage" on the roll paper. Explain that a collage is a type of art project that is a collection of many different things.
- Distribute the materials and make sure each child has a space to work on the paper; point out the glue and say something like *I wonder what our collage will look like.*

Middle

- Talk with children about the properties of the objects in their collection (e.g., size, shape, color, texture, lines, design).

- Talk about the aesthetic properties of the materials (e.g., hue or intensity of color, texture, matte or shiny surface), specific areas of the collage, and the collage as a whole. Use art-related vocabulary to talk about the arrangement of objects, use of space, color, and textural contrasts (e.g., *This area of the collage has lots of objects crowded close together, but over here they are very spread out; Your eye can follow this line of shells across the page* [trace line with fingers].
- Introduce backup collage materials and say *Here are some other materials you might want to use in the collage.*

End

- Ask children where they would like to hang their collage. Encourage them to show and talk about the collage with family members at drop-off and pickup times.
- Put all the extra materials in one container (or sort them into separate containers) and store them in the art area for children who want to make collage(s) at work/choice time.
- Have each child choose one item and use it as the basis for transitioning to the next activity (e.g., *Whoever chose a pine cone, go to* [the next activity]; *Whoever picked a pebble, go to* [the next activity]).

Ideas for follow-up

- Take a picture of the collages and post them on the parent bulletin board (or include them in the family newsletter). Encourage parents to collect natural objects with children and make collages at home.
- Bring in art books and reproductions of collages; talk about the materials used and the arrangements made by the artists.

- Repeat the activity but give each child his/her own piece of paper or a paper plate to make a collage.
- Play a sorting game with the children using the items collected from outside.

Adaptations for children with special needs

- If children cannot work on the floor, give them individual pieces of paper at the table or on their wheelchair trays.
- If children are concerned about using the glue due to sensory sensitivity, provide plastic gloves.

Children can choose to work individually or collaboratively to create collages with natural objects gathered on a class walk.

Developmental range: Supporting children at different levels

Earlier ⟶

Children may

- Play with the objects collected but not try to glue them onto the collage (e.g., they may move them around on the paper or on the floor, sort them into piles, make up a story about them).
- Play with the glue (e.g., dab or squeeze it on their fingers, put it on the paper, spread it with their hands).
- Glue one or two objects to the paper.

Adults can

- Explore the objects (e.g., arrange, sort), following the children's lead; describe their own actions and those of the children; refer to the names and properties of the objects (e.g., *I'm putting my leaves and pine cones in separate piles, just like you*).
- Encourage children to describe what they are doing with the glue and how it feels (e.g., *You're spreading the glue with your fingers. How does it feel?*).
- Say, *I wonder if you are going to glue anything else to the collage.* If the child indicates yes, say *Show me what you will use next.*

Middle ⟶

Children may

- Glue several objects onto the paper but do not try to arrange them in any way.
- Talk about why they chose certain objects (e.g., *It feels smooth; This is green — I like green*).
- Glue objects onto the paper and say their collage looks like something specific (e.g., *It's the birds we saw on the telephone wire*).

Adults can

- Talk to children about the items they chose to glue on the collage (e.g., *I wonder why you chose to use them*).
- Acknowledge, support, and extend children's statements about collecting and/or using the objects (e.g., *I remember when Delia found the acorn. She let you put it in your basket; Can I feel it too? It is really smooth!*).
- Encourage children to sort, arrange, and describe the objects in their collections.

Later ⟶

Children may

- Deliberately arrange objects on paper (e.g., glue a leaf surrounded by a circle of pine cones).
- Say the glued objects form some type of representation (e.g., *These* [child points to twigs] *are the arms*); say they are going to make something specific (e.g., a shape, object, person) and proceed to do so (e.g., *I'm going to glue a kitty*).
- Glue objects in a sequence or pattern and describe the pattern (e.g., *I glued a rock, a leaf, a rock, a leaf*).
- Describe aesthetic properties of their area of the collage or the collage as a whole (e.g., *I made it bumpy here and smooth here; We made a really crowded collage!*).

Adults can

- Talk with children about the objects they chose and how they decided to make their arrangements (e.g., *I wonder why you used all the shells but only one twig*).
- Ask children to describe the representations they've created.
- Encourage children to describe their patterns, and copy them (e.g., *Tell me what goes next*).
- Talk about the aesthetic properties of the materials and the collage; repeat children's words and add new vocabulary words (e.g., *white space, arrangement, contrasting colors*).

45 Recycled Materials and Three-dimensional Constructions

Children use scrap and recycled materials to create multidimensional structures.

Time of day: Small-Group Time

Content Area: The Arts: Visual Art

Materials

Materials for each child and teacher:

- Variety of scrap and recycled materials (e.g., plastic containers, foam shapes, Styrofoam packing materials, Popsicle sticks, cardboard tubes)
- Cardboard boxes
- Masking tape and scissors

Shared materials:

- None

Backup materials:

- Yarn, pipe cleaners
- Materials for decorating boxes and constructions (e.g., markers, crayons, stickers)

Beginning

- Give each child a set of materials and say something like *Some of you have been building things in the block area and woodworking area. Here are lots of materials you can use to build and construct things. I wonder what kind of things you can build with them.*

Middle

- Describe and encourage children to describe the materials they are using and what they are doing with them. Repeat their words and introduce new vocabulary words (e.g., *stacking,* *mounting, constructing, two-* and *three-dimensional*). Use words related to size, shape, and spatial relationships (e.g., *next to, on top of/above, below/underneath, side by side, raised/flat, higher/lower*).
- Use the materials in the same way the children do; ask for their assistance (e.g., suggest they demonstrate for you how to do what they are doing, or ask for verbal instructions).
- Refer children to one another for collaboration and problem-solving (e.g., suggest that one holds while another tapes).
- Introduce backup materials if children want to incorporate these into their structures or use them for decoration.

End

- Ask children where and how to display their structures (e.g., on a shelf, on carton "pedestals"). Encourage them to share their structures with parents at drop-off and pickup times. Some children may choose to take their projects home.
- Remind children where materials will be stored so that if they choose, they can continue building with them at work/choice time.
- Ask children to roll "like a roll of tape" to the next activity (or) to pretend they have sticky tape on the bottoms of their shoes!

Ideas for follow-up

- At outside time, take children for a walk to look at the different structures and buildings in the neighborhood.
- Bring in books, architecture magazines, and other printed materials with pictures of different kinds of buildings. Bring in art books and reproductions of sculptures made of recycled materials.

Adaptations for children with special needs

- Prepare precut strips of tape for children who have trouble with fine motor coordination.
- Encourage children with visual limitations to touch and feel the construction materials; focus on size, shape, and texture.

Using scissors and tape can be as interesting to children as exploring recycled and other materials in constructing a three-dimensional collage.

Developmental range: Supporting children at different levels

Earlier ⟶   **Middle** ⟶   **Later** ⟶

Earlier

Children may

- Play with the construction materials, boxes, or tape (e.g., nest, sort, or align boxes; peel tape off the roll or roll it into little balls).
- Use the scissors to cut materials but not assemble them into a construction.
- Tape two materials together.
- Make a construction and then notice it looks like something familiar (e.g., *This is my apartment. I live in the middle with my mom and grammy*).

Adults can

- Use materials in the same way the child does (e.g., stack containers, sort or line up materials).
- Refer the child to another child who has mastered how to use the tape (e.g., *I see that Ming is using the tape. Ask her how she got it off the roll*).
- Notice similarities between materials and familiar objects (e.g., *This tube reminds me of our tunnel slide on the playground*).
- Describe and encourage children to describe the materials and shapes they are cutting.
- Acknowledge when/how children combine materials (e.g., *You taped together the cardboard tube and the stick*).

Middle

Children may

- Wrap or decorate a container with the tape.
- Make a simple construction with one or two details (e.g., tape two sticks in a cross and stick one end in a paper towel tube).
- Give their construction a name or label (e.g., *This is my spy tube*).
- Say they are going to make something and explain how (e.g., *I'm going to build a snow fort with this box and cotton balls*), then proceed to construct it.

Adults can

- Comment on how children have wrapped or decorated their box (e.g., *You wrapped yellow yarn 'round and 'round the sides; Here's a pattern with red and blue dots*).
- Comment on the nature or number of materials children use (e.g., *You built something with two sticks and a cardboard tube; You used 1…2… 3…4 boxes in your tower!*).
- Ask children to describe the parts of what they created (e.g., *Tell me about this tall piece that sticks up in the air*).
- Ask children if their construction is similar to other items in the room. Look around the room with the child and talk about similarities and differences (e.g., in size, shape, texture).

Later

Children may

- Make a complex construction with three or more details (e.g., tape Popsicle sticks around the top of a carton, fill it with Styrofoam and upright tubes, and put a pipe cleaner in each tube).
- Name or describe something they have created (e.g., *This is my robot — his feet, arms, hands, pinching reachers, and here's where the battery goes*).
- Problem-solve with the materials (e.g., try unsuccessfully to attach something with one piece of tape, then reposition it and use several pieces of crossed tape so it will hold).
- Use the backup materials to add details (e.g., *I need more yarn. My robot needs hair on his whole head, not just on the front*).

Adults can

- Ask children if they are going to add anything else to their constructions or what they plan to do next.
- Ask children how they made their structures (e.g., which materials they used, how they got materials to balance or stick together).
- Acknowledge the sequence of steps children used to solve a problem (e.g., *First you tried taping the small box to the side, then balancing it, and then you put another box under it to stabilize and hold it in place*).
- Encourage children to collaborate to solve a problem (e.g., *I wonder if it would work if two of you did that together*).

46 Exploring Instruments

Children use a variety of instruments in different ways to make and compare sounds.

Time of day: Small-Group Time

Content Area: The Arts: Music

Materials

Materials for each child and teacher:

- None

Shared materials:

- A variety of instruments, such as tambourines, rhythm sticks, maracas, cymbals, small drums, bells, triangles, sand blocks, tone blocks

Backup materials:

- Extra instruments

Beginning

- Say *Today in our small group we are going to move to an area of the classroom where we can sit on the floor and have more room.*
- When every one is seated, pass out the instruments so each child and adult has one and say, *Today for small-group time I thought it would be fun to play these instruments. Let's see what kinds of music or sounds we can make with them.*

Middle

- Imitate how children use the instruments.
- Talk to children about how they are using the instruments and the sounds they are making. Use descriptive words for their actions (e.g., *shaking, banging, pounding, rubbing*) and the variety of sounds they make (e.g., *loud/soft, high/low, humming, tinkly, pinging, rough/smooth*).
- Encourage children to try making the same sounds with their mouths, or hands and feet.
- Challenge children to play their instruments loudly and softly and to make a sound "in between" loud and soft.

- Midway through the activity, ask children to switch instruments with one another and/or introduce backup instruments, so they can explore more sounds (if children prefer not to switch, let them continue using the instrument they have).

End

- Ask children to march as if they are in a marching band to the next part of the daily routine.

Ideas for follow-up

- For large-group time the next day, have the children form a marching band with the instruments.
- At outside time, encourage children to listen to outdoor sounds (e.g., animals, machines, car horns) and compare them to the sounds made by the instruments.
- Use instruments to signal warnings for transitions by playing or having a child play an instrument five minutes before cleanup. Have children take turns choosing and playing an instrument on different days.

Adaptations for children with special needs

- Assist children with visual impairments, allowing them to feel their instruments before playing them. Encourage them to feel the vibrations as they play.
- Help children with physical impairments to hold instruments in a way that is most comfortable for them as they play. If necessary, hold instruments for them or anchor them in place. Encourage other children to assist peers with disabilities in holding their instruments.

Developmental range: Supporting children at different levels

Earlier →

Children may
- Watch and listen to peers play their instruments.
- Imitate the way another person (adult or child) plays an instrument.
- Play one instrument consistently the same way.

Adults can
- Describe the sound(s) made by the instrument the children are listening to or playing; encourage children to describe what they hear.
- Comment that child is playing his/her instrument the same way as ___ (adult or another child). Describe what the child is doing (e.g., *You're shaking the tambourine just like Wanda is shaking the bell*).
- Play follow the leader with children, using an instrument in different ways as children follow. Invite them to be the leader and imitate what they do.

Middle →

Children may
- Play one instrument in more than one way (e.g., shaking, banging with hand or wooden stick).
- Play more than one instrument in more than one way.
- Describe an action or sound in simple terms (e.g., *I shook it; It's loud*).

Adults can
- Ask children if they can think of other ways to play the instruments.
- Encourage children to try different instruments and compare the sounds they make.
- Ask children to describe their actions and the sounds of their instruments. Repeat children's words and add new vocabulary.
- Have children pass their instruments to the next person when they hear a key word (such as the name of a person, an instrument, an object, or even a nonsense word). Ask children to suggest key words.

Later →

Children may
- Suggest different ways to play the instruments and/or make different types of sounds (on head, behind back; soft, loud).
- Describe an action or sound related to an instrument in complex terms (e.g., *I'm holding it in my lap and hitting it with both hands; It's like the loud gong at my temple; The triangle sounds soft and tinkly*).
- Attempt to duplicate a sound with their voice or body movements (e.g., make a humming noise; clap hands to imitate the sound of banging two wooden blocks together).
- Sing a song as they play their instruments.

Adults can
- Call children's attention to the ways others are using their instruments (e.g., *Cassie is shaking her maracas high in the air; Johann is hitting the drum very softly*). Encourage children to imitate and elaborate on one another's actions.
- Acknowledge all the ways children are exploring actions and sounds with the instruments.
- Challenge children to try playing their instruments in different positions or using different techniques (e.g., shaking, banging, tapping).
- Encourage children to make different types of sounds with their instruments (e.g., high/low, soft/loud, fast/slow, rough/smooth).
- Make up songs to go with the sounds and rhythms children produce, using familiar melodies (e.g., "Row Your Boat") or inventing simple tunes. Encourage children to contribute their ideas.

Playing instruments and exploring sounds involves many senses and is equally appealing to children of different developmental and ability levels.

47 Making Musical Shakers

Children fill small metal containers with dried beans, beads, and similar items to create musical shakers that produce a variety of sounds.

Time of day: Small-Group Time

Content Area: The Arts: Music

Materials

Materials for each child and teacher:

- Empty metal containers such as small round tins, Altoid tins, metal nut cans with plastic lids, or any small metallic container with a closeable lid (Note: As a safety precaution, carefully run your finger around the tops of metal cans and lids to make certain there are no jagged edges.)
- Items to fill the containers (e.g., dried beans, small beads or buttons, pebbles, bells, small shells)
- Thick tape (masking or duct); scissors

Shared materials:

- None

Backup materials:

- Assortment of craft items for decorating the shakers (e.g., markers, crayons; stickers, foam shapes; glue sticks)

Beginning

- Distribute the materials to each child and say something like *At large-group time yesterday, we shook the maracas to music. Here are some materials to make your own shakers.*

Middle

- Problem-solve with children about how to put the shakers together. Gather and support their ideas; help them think of alternatives if necessary. For example, if a child wants to glue the lid onto the container, you might say, *Glue can take a long time to dry and then you would have to wait to use your shaker. See if there's something else you can use to seal your tin shut.*

- Assist children if necessary, or refer them to one another for help. Allow children to problem-solve and carry out their ideas on their own as much as possible (e.g., if a child is trying to cut a piece of tape, you might say something like *I can hold the tape while you cut,* or *I can hold the tin while you wrap the tape around it.*

- Once children have filled and sealed their shakers, talk with them about the different sounds the shakers make and why. Introduce vocabulary words related to sound (e.g., loud and soft; high and low; fast and slow; jumpy and smooth).

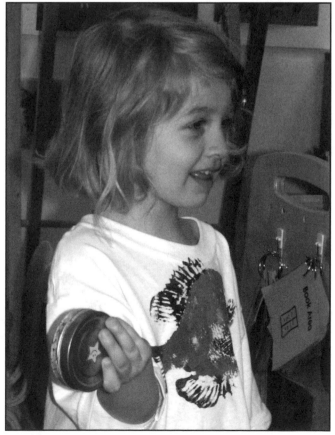

Children can create their musical shakers using a variety of fillers and compare the different sounds they make.

- For children who finish more quickly than others, bring out the backup materials so they can decorate their shakers.
- Have children decide how to write their name or draw their letter-linked picture or symbol on their shaker so they know which one is theirs.

End

- Talk with children about leaving their shakers at school for use during large-group time, work/choice time, and other parts of the day; discuss where the shakers should be stored. Remind children that they can plan to make another shaker at work/choice time if they'd like to take one home.
- Have children throw away any scraps and sort/organize extra materials into separate containers.
- After children store their shakers, have them "shake" their bodies to the next activity.

Ideas for follow-up

- Use the shakers at large-group time.
- Put the shakers in a container, label it, and put it in the area of the classroom where the instruments are stored.

- Use the shakers at planning or recall time. For example, at planning time, pick out one of the children's shakers from a large basket; whomever it belongs to plans next. At recall time, children who are recalling can go to the area where they worked and shake their shaker while others in the group close their eyes and guess which area of the classroom the sound is coming from. Then the child who is recalling returns to the group and shares what he or she did during work/choice time. Continue in this way until every child has the opportunity to plan (or recall).

Adaptations for children with special needs

- Encourage children with visual and/or motor limitations to explore the sounds made by different fillers and containers. Ask them to tell you (or another child) which of the filler items they want to put in their shakers.

Developmental range: Supporting children at different levels

Earlier →

Children may

- Put beans in an open container (e.g., one half of tin) and begin shaking it around.
- Ask for help getting tape off the roll.
- Explore tape (e.g., roll it in a ball, place beans on tape).
- Ask for help taping the two halves of the shaker together.
- Decorate the shaker without a specific design in mind.

Adults can

- Describe what the children are doing with the beans and tins (e.g., *You are excited and want to shake the beans now; You got the beans to stick to the tape*).
- Refer children to one another for help with getting tape off the roll.
- Comment on how children have decorated their shaker (e.g., *You made swirly marks all around the bottom*).

Middle →

Children may

- Act with intention to make their shaker (e.g., choose the container and filler after trying more than one combination, concentrating on each step).
- Describe and compare the sounds made by different containers and fillers; express a preference (e.g., *The beans are too loud. I like it better with the rice inside*).
- Problem-solve with materials in one or two ways (e.g., try to pull the tape apart to untangle it, then cut another piece).
- Describe the sound of their shaker (e.g., *Mine's really loud 'cause I used lots of beans; His sounds funny 'cause it's smaller than mine*).

Adults can

- Talk with children about what they need to do first to make their shakers; ask what they will do next.
- Refer children to one another for help with assembling their shakers (e.g., *Amy got her tins together. You could ask her how she did it*).
- Acknowledge children's efforts, and encourage their ideas (e.g., *I see you got the tin together by taping it from top to bottom; Jarett filled his with pebbles instead of beans*).
- Talk with children about how the different fillers sound in the different containers (e.g., *Yours has a higher pitch and his has a deeper pitch*).

Later →

Children may

- Manipulate materials with greater skill (e.g., place beans in tin; put halves of tin together; pull tape off roll; cut tape with scissors and place it around tin).
- Describe the materials and steps they use to make their shakers (e.g., name materials; say or count out how many beans go inside the tin; describe wrapping the tape around the middle).
- Have a design in mind for placing decorations on their shakers.

Adults can

- Talk with children about how they want to decorate their shaker. Point out any patterns or specific designs (e.g., *You only used pink stickers for your shaker; I see you put a blue sticker, then a green sticker, then a blue sticker. What will come next?*).
- Ask children to predict how different fillers will sound in different containers; encourage them to explain their reasoning (e.g., *Pamela has a tall can and you have a short can. I wonder how the beans will sound in yours compared to hers?; Why do you think the pebbles will sound louder than the shells?*).

48 Making Sounds With Everyday Objects

Children explore a variety of ordinary objects to make and describe different sounds.

Time of day: Small-Group Time

Content Area: The Arts: Music

Materials

Materials for each child and teacher:

- Everyday objects that can be used to make different sounds (e.g., combs, spoons, Styrofoam cups, pop cans, small plastic juice containers, large binder clips, a set of keys, craft sticks, pebbles, small cardboard boxes, Velcro tabs, small bells, chains, and whistles)

Shared materials:

- None

Backup materials:

- Masking tape

Beginning

- Say *Here are some things that make different sounds.* Choose and name two or three objects and demonstrate the sounds they make (e.g., run your finger across the teeth of a comb, shake two pebbles together in your cupped hands, pull apart the pieces of a Velcro tab).
- Distribute the materials to each child and say *I wonder what kinds of sounds you can make with these things.*

Middle

- Name and encourage children to name and talk about the objects they use and the sounds they make. Accept their words and add new vocabulary (e.g., *whistles, bells, the things you use to open the door, snap, ding-dong, scritch-scratch*).

- Midway through the activity, introduce the masking tape and say *I wonder what kinds of sounds these items will make if you tape some of them together.* Demonstrate by taping two objects together and manipulating them in different ways (e.g., shaking, rubbing, blowing), and talk with the children about the resulting sound; discuss how it is different from the individual sounds each object made on its own. Encourage children to try different combinations. (If necessary, help them problem-solve to tear strips off the roll of tape and/or tape objects together.)

End

- Put the materials in one large basket and ask the children for suggestions about where to store it for work/choice time the next day should they want to explore more sounds.
- Ask children to make a quiet sound on the way to the next activity.

Ideas for follow-up

- Have a "sound hunt" to look for things in the room that may have or make a sound and to explore how to produce or hear the sound.
- Call attention to everyday (environmental) sounds children hear indoors and outdoors (e.g., fire truck, squeaky door, cabinet doors opening and closing, lawnmower, airplane, emergency vehicles). Ask them to identify the source of the sound.

Adaptations for children with special needs

• For children with hearing limitations, be sure to include objects that make loud sounds and/or vibrate.

• Encourage children with visual limitations to feel the parts of the objects that produce sounds, such as the teeth of a comb; the difference between the surfaces of metal, wood, and plastic; or the texture of the two halves of a Velcro tab.

In this small group, children explore the sounds made by everyday objects, alone or in combination. Here they beat together familiar items made of wood, plastic, and/or metal.

Developmental range: Supporting children at different levels

Earlier ⟶

Children may
- Play or pretend with the objects but not explore their sounds.
- Choose the same objects as and/or imitate the actions of others (e.g., shake a bell or bang two spoons together as the teacher or another child does).
- Use only objects they know make sounds (e.g., keys, bells).

Adults can
- Use objects to make sounds and say to the children, *I wonder what sounds the items in your basket can make.*
- Acknowledge how children are imitating actions and sounds (e.g., *You're banging together two spoons and making the same loud noise as Tammy*).
- Encourage children to explore more objects (e.g., *I wonder if any of the other things also make sounds*).

Middle ⟶

Children may
- Use different objects in different ways (e.g., pound cup against the table open side up and open side down).
- Express surprise at some sounds or that some objects make sounds (e.g., *Hey, these boxes make noise if you rub them together. Listen!*).
- Tape two or more items together to make new or different sounds.

Adults can
- Use the objects to make sounds similar to those children are making.
- Talk to the children about the sounds they are making. Repeat their words and add new vocabulary words.
- Ask children how they made a particular sound and copy them (e.g., *Can you tell me how you did that? Do you think I could make the same sound with the cups? How do you suppose I could do that?*).
- Ask children to create names for new items they make by taping objects together.

Later ⟶

Children may
- Describe their actions and/or the resulting sounds (e.g., *I rubbed it on the table real fast to make a noise; It spits when you run your finger across the top*).
- Compare sounds they make or hear to everyday sounds or familiar instruments (e.g., *I can make it go ticktock like a clock; It's a train whistle; Jimmy plays his drums just the same way. Kaboom, kaboom, bam!*).
- Compare two or more sounds (e.g., *This cup* [plastic] *is louder than this one* [Styrofoam]; *The chain is not as loud as the key when you shake it in the cup*).

Adults can
- Ask children if a sound reminds them of anything else they are familiar with.
- Say, *Let's each make a sound and see if we can figure out which one is louder/softer* [higher/lower, etc.].
- Ask children to predict what kind of sound an object will make.
- Tape two objects together and ask children to predict if/ how it will sound different from each of the individual objects.
- Keep a steady beat with sounds children make, and repeat a word to emphasize the beat (e.g., shake, shake, shake; tap, tap, tap); encourage children to choose a word to repeat.

49 Musical Patterns

Children listen to music with a simple beat and tap out patterns, imitating the teacher's and then creating their own.

Time of day: Small-Group Time | **Content Area:** The Arts: Music

Materials

Materials for each child and teacher:
- None

Shared materials:
- CD of instrumental music familiar to the children; music should have a simple beat (e.g., four beats to the measure; selection should be long enough to last for many repeats and/or have additional selections with a comparable simple beat)

Backup materials:
- None

Beginning

- Sit on the floor with the children and start the music. (This activity can also be done at the table or outdoors.)
- Pat your hands first on the floor and then on your knees. After tapping the pattern a couple of times, say *floor, knees, floor, knees, floor, knees* as you tap. Encourage the children to pat the pattern with you as they also say the words. Repeat the pattern at least a dozen times (six or more musical measures).
- Tell the children that what they are doing makes a pattern because they are patting the same two places over and over, repeating the same action each time. Say *Let's see what other patterns we can pat.*

Middle

- Ask one of the children to suggest two places to pat (e.g., foot and head). Say and pat the pattern with the children.
- Continue asking children to suggest two places to pat until each child who wants to contribute an idea has a turn. (Do not require children to take a turn.)

- Use the word *pattern* and pattern-related language (e.g., *We're making a pattern because we keep patting the same two places. It's a pattern because it repeats over and over again.*
- Say each pattern aloud. Use your voice to emphasize when each repeat begins (e.g., **knees,** *floor;* **knees,** *floor;* **knees,** *floor*).
- When the music ends, restart the same music or change to another selection with a simple beat so children can easily pat a pattern.
- Once the activity is established, ask children to make their own patterns. Move among the children, imitating the patterns they create; encouraging them to verbalize their patterns; and suggesting they watch and copy one another's patterns.

End

- Give children a warning before you do the last pattern. Ask them to suggest the number of repetitions they would like to do.
- Create a movement pattern to transition to the next activity (e.g., *big jump, little jump; big jump, little jump; big jump, little jump*). Say the pattern aloud as children move to the next location.

Ideas for follow-up

- Use movement patterns at transitions (e.g., to help children settle down when they first assemble for large-group time; to facilitate moving from message board to planning tables).
- Together with the children, generate movement patterns from different body positions (e.g., sitting or lying on the floor; while standing; sitting in a chair).

Adaptations for children with special needs

- For children with auditory limitations, choose musical selections that allow them to feel/hear vibrations (e.g., music with a loud bass line). Add supplementary visual cues, such as nodding your head or swaying your body to the beat, visually emphasizing the beginning of each pattern repetition.

- For children with visual limitations, describe and emphasize the pattern repetitions with your voice. Sit near them so they can hear and feel where you pat. Encourage children to join in saying the pattern aloud.

- Encourage children with motor limitations to create patterns with whatever body part(s) they can easily move. Prop them on the floor with pillows so their arms are free to pat; children can also sit in and pat parts of their wheelchairs.

In this activity, teachers tap out and say a simple two-part pattern for children to imitate. Children then take turns as leaders, creating patterns for others to imitate.

Developmental range: Supporting children at different levels

Earlier →

Children may

- Tap different parts of their bodies in random sequence (e.g., head, toes, knees, elbows, head, stomach).
- Tap and name two places once but not continue the pattern.
- Copy the first two steps (*AB*) of a sequence created by the teacher or another child but not carry out the pattern.
- Copy an *ABABAB* pattern initiated by the teacher or another child; do at least three repetitions.
- Tap one or more places and ask the teacher if they did a pattern (e.g., tap head, toes, head and say, *Did I do a pattern?*).

Adults can

- Copy the sequences a child makes (random or patterned). Use the word *pattern* when appropriate.
- Create a pattern and encourage children to copy it. Do it together with them.
- Tap children's pattern and say the names of the places they tap; emphasize the beginning of each repetition (e.g., *Nita tapped her head and her tummy. Let's make a pattern: head, tummy, head, tummy, head, tummy*). Encourage children to tap and say the pattern with you.

Middle →

Children may

- Say the words while copying a pattern (e.g., *knees, toes, knees, toes, knees, toes*).
- Create a pattern by patting two places at least three times.
- Watch to see if others correctly copy the pattern they have made; correct other's mistakes (e.g., *No, Stephen. You have to do* nose, ear).
- Say they are doing a pattern but not say what makes it a pattern (e.g., *I made a pattern. Now you try it!*).
- Copy an *AABB* or *AAB* pattern; repeat the pattern at least three times.

Adults can

- Talk about patting the same two places over and over again, exploring the idea that patterns repeat the same elements in the same sequence (e.g., *We're tapping our noses and our shoulders over and over again. That's what makes it a pattern*).
- Introduce an *AABBAABB-AABB* pattern for the children to copy (e.g., *Now I'm going to pat a different way: head, head, shoulders, shoulders; head, head, shoulders, shoulders; head, head, shoulders, shoulders. Try it with me*). Encourage children to copy and say the pattern aloud.
- Encourage children to create an *AABBAABBAABB* pattern (e.g., *Let's see if you can make a pattern like mine. I tapped one place twice, then another place twice, then back to first place twice, and the second place twice. The same two places, two times, over and over*).

Later →

Children may

- Identify the patting sequence as a pattern; say what makes a pattern a pattern (e.g., *Look at my pattern. I'm doing* knees, toes, knees, toes *over and over again*).
- Extend someone else's pattern by saying where to tap next (e.g., *We gotta touch our noses next. Noses go after elbows every time*).
- Create an *AABB* or *AAB* pattern.
- Create a three-element pattern (e.g., *ABCABCABC*).

Adults can

- Create an *AABAABAAB* or *ABBABBABB* pattern using children's ideas about where to tap, and encourage children to copy it. Say the pattern aloud together with the children.
- Stop patting and ask children, *Where do I pat next?*
- Make a mistake (e.g., pat knees, toes, knees, toes, knees, knees). If children do not correct you, say *Oops. That doesn't look right. Can you see what I did wrong?* Encourage them to offer suggestions for "fixing" the pattern.
- Create sequences (random or patterned) and ask children whether these sequences are patterns (e.g., knees, toes, toes; knees, knees, knees). Ask what does (or does not) make each a pattern.

50 Our Group's Songs

Children sing songs together, then suggest and sing variations and extensions.

Time of day: Small-Group Time   **Content Area:** The Arts: Music

Materials

Materials for each child and teacher:

- Song book cards (small picture cards of the songs in the class song book)

Shared materials:

- Chart paper and markers

Backup materials:

- Tape recorder

Beginning

- Distribute song book cards and say *Today we are going to sing songs. Here are small picture cards of the songs in our song book. Look through them and choose a song you would like us all to sing.*

Middle

- Taking turns, sing the songs each child chooses. Depending on the length of the song, sing it through once or twice.
- After each song is completed, ask children to suggest different ways to sing it (e.g., by adding a verse [extension], changing the last word of a line or singing it higher/lower [variation]).
- Write on poster board the words that you change or the pictures you will add to or change on the cards when extending or varying a song.

End

- Let children know when you are singing the last song of the activity, and ask for ideas on where to hang the song poster in the room.
- Ask children to suggest a variation on the last song and to sing on the way to the next part of the routine.

Ideas for follow-up

- Use song storybooks such as "Frog Went A-Courtin'," "Old MacDonald," and "Down in the Meadow" to sing at large-group time or at another small-group time.
- Encourage children to add/draw additional variations to the class song book.
- Sing songs and variations at transition times.

Adaptations for children with special needs

- For children with auditory limitations, accompany words with movements.
- For children with visual limitations, use large print and pictures in the song book and on song cards and chart paper.

In this activity, children sing songs in the class song book, and then suggest different ways to sing them by adding verses, changing words, or varying the pitch or loudness.

Developmental range: Supporting children at different levels

Earlier →

Children may
- Choose a song by holding up a song card; not name or describe the words in the song.
- Hum along with the song.
- Sing some of the words with the group.
- Move their body along with the song.

Adults can
- Name the song on the card the child holds up (e.g., *You want to sing* "Twinkle, Twinkle, Little Star").
- Hum along with children who are humming.
- Acknowledge when children are singing some of the words (e.g., nod or smile; say *You were singing along with the boat song and the star song!*).
- Imitate children's movements to the songs.

Middle →

Children may
- Choose a song and identify it by name or key words (e.g., hold up the card and say, *I want to sing the* spider *song*).
- Sing songs the way they've heard them or sung them before, without variations or extensions.
- Identify the name or content of a song chosen by another child after hearing the first few words (e.g., *I know that. It's the MacDonald farm song!*).

Adults can
- Ask children to suggest other ways the group can sing the song (e.g., *How would the song sound if a giant or a baby was singing it?*).
- Acknowledge when children recognize a song (e.g., *You knew what we were singing as soon as you heard the first two words!*).
- Begin by singing the wrong song or sing it incorrectly and see if children correct you. If not, say *That doesn't sound right. How should it go?*

Later →

Children may
- Suggest a way to extend a song (e.g., *What if Old MacDonald also has a ghost on his farm and it goes boo, boo?*).
- Suggest a way to vary a song (e.g., *I want to sing my favorite song but in a quiet mousy voice; This time make the spider go up a tree*).
- Suggest a way to represent the change (extension or variation) on the chart paper (e.g., *Draw a spider crawling up a tree*).

Adults can
- Ask children to suggest variations of the song (e.g., *How could we make the song longer* [or shorter]?; *What other words can we sing to this music?*).
- Make a list of the words children will substitute in the songs.
- Ask children to suggest a way of representing (writing or drawing) the changes they suggest for the chart poster.

51 Painting to Music

Children paint designs on paper while listening to different types of music.

Time of day: Small-Group Time

Content Area: The Arts: Music

Materials

Materials for each child and teacher:

- 1 color of paint
- Paintbrushes
- Smock

Shared materials:

- One long piece of roll paper (if you do not have large roll paper, then give each child one large piece of paper)
- Various types of instrumental music (e.g., loud, soft, slow, fast, gentle, percussive)

Backup materials:

- One other color of paint or a different type of brush for each child

Beginning

- Have children get a smock to protect their clothing while you clear a space on the floor for the paper and for all of the children to gather around it and paint.
- Say *We are going to paint today, but while we are painting I am going to play some music. It may be fast or slow or loud or soft. As you listen to the music, think about how the music makes you feel while you are painting. I wonder if the music will make you paint in different ways.*
- Pass out paint and paintbrushes. Begin to play the first selection of music.

Middle

- Play each type of music for at least one to two minutes before changing to another selection.
- Converse with children about how they feel as they are listening to the music and painting at the same time (e.g., *I wonder how this music is making you feel; When you listen to the mu-*

sic, you can hear the flutes. How do the flutes make you want to move your paintbrush?; I see you are making circular movements with your hands when you hear the soft music; Jeremy, you began moving your brush up and down quickly when the fast music came on).

- Some children prefer not to talk when they are doing artwork. Respect their desire for silence. Sit next to them and observe and/or imitate what they are doing. Wait to see if a child initiates a conversation; if not, continue to provide silent support.
- If children ask for additional materials, introduce another color of paint or a different (thicker or thinner) brush.

End

- Put on a final selection of music and let children know it is the last one. Have children move to the next activity based on how the music makes them feel.

Ideas for follow-up

- Display the children's painting after it dries, and talk with them about their artwork. Explore with children the differences in the various designs and how specific designs might correspond to the different kinds of music they heard. Encourage children to show the group painting to their parents at dropoff and pick-up time and to talk to them about it.
- Use different types of music but change the media you use (e.g., two colors of paint, fingerpaint, water colors; eye droppers, string, sponges, toothbrushes; different types of paper/cardstock). Children can also paint using parts of their body, such as their feet, hands, and/or elbows.

- Do this activity outdoors along with music, and give children child-sized brooms or brushes and pails of water to paint with on the pavement.

Adaptations for children with special needs

- Support children with auditory limitations as they feel and paint to the vibrations of the music.
- Encourage children with visual limitations to move their bodies to the music.

Children listen to different types of music and "paint" the way it makes them feel on a shared roll of paper. Children may also describe the music, their feelings, and the images they paint.

Developmental range: Supporting children at different levels

Earlier →

Children may
- Fill in an entire area of the paper with paint; may apply so much paint or rub brush so hard they make a hole in the paper.
- Use fingers or hands to paint on paper; paint on hands.
- Make simple marks and lines on paper with paintbrush.
- Move parts of their body as they listen to the music (e.g., bob head up and down, pat thigh, move toes or tap feet, hit paper with paintbrush in time to music).

Adults can
- Use the materials and imitate the children's actions.
- Comment on children's painting (e.g., *You filled that whole space with paint; Those are long lines that you painted!*).
- Comment on children's movements as they listen to the music. Join them. Gently pat the beat in time to their movements (but stop if this distracts them from painting).
- Ask children about their feelings as they listen to the music. Share feelings about and comment on the music (e.g., *This music sounds happy to me. What about you?*).

Middle →

Children may
- Be purposeful about what they are painting; describe it in simple language (e.g., *I'm making circles*).
- Make a simple statement connecting what they are painting to the music (e.g., *This makes me go fast*).
- Paint an image or design to correspond to the feel of the music; make a simple statement connecting the music and feelings (e.g., *This is sad music so I'm painting all frowns*).

Adults can
- Talk about the designs children make (e.g., *It's a row of circles; It's thin on top and thick on the bottom*).
- Discuss with children how the music makes them feel and how it is connected to their painting (e.g., *I wonder if you made this design when the fast music was on; There were lots of drums in this music. Did the drums make you pound the paint on the paper?*).

Later →

Children may
- Make a more complex painting with three or more details (e.g., make a box, fill it with dots and stars, and then thicken the border).
- Describe in detail what they are painting and feeling; elaborate with a reason (e.g., *I'm painting flowers 'cause the music is happy and so are flowers; This sounds scary. Look at my scary face*).
- Paint with another child and collaborate on what they are painting. Talk to each other about the music and painting (e.g., *Look, yours is squiggly and you went fast to the music. Now let's go slow*).

Adults can
- Refer children to one another to share their paintings and to talk about the feelings they had when they made them.
- Talk with children about the details of their paintings and discuss the different types of music. Introduce new vocabulary words to describe the music and their artwork (e.g., *This music is called* jazz. *How does it make you feel?; What kind of music was playing when you made this design with lots of dots close together? Musicians call those short notes* staccato. *I saw you painting fast while you were listening to it*).
- Comment on how children share and build on one another's ideas.

52 Sing It Like...

Children create variations of familiar songs by adopting the voices and movements of different people, characters, and objects.

Time of day: Small-Group Time

Content Area: The Arts: Music

Materials

Materials for each child and teacher:
• None

Shared materials:
• Classroom song book

Backup materials:
• None

Beginning

• Sing a familiar song with the children (such as "Row, Row, Row Your Boat" or another song the children enjoy singing). After you sing it together two or three times through, say *I wonder how this song would sound if we sang it like a baby would?* Listen to and discuss the children's ideas (e.g., *It would sound like* waa, waa, waa; *A baby can't sing the words but maybe it could hum; Really, really high*). Then say *Let's sing "Row, Row, Row Your Boat" as a baby might.* Sing it two or three times, using the children's suggestions.

• Encourage the children to sing the song in the voice/character of someone or something else (e.g., *Can you sing it like a kitty cat? A race car driver? A shark?*). Make suggestions based on children's interests you have observed during work/choice time.

• Ask *How else could we sing "Row, Row, Row Your Boat"?* Listen to and discuss the children's ideas and then sing the song in whatever ways they suggest (e.g., *We can sing it like the Papa Bear, the Mama Bear, and the Baby Bear; Let's sing it like my daddy — he has a really low voice*).

Middle

• Ask for more suggestions from children on characters/objects they might adopt to sing the song, and try their ideas. Describe and encourage them to describe voice quality, using terms such as *pitch* (higher, lower), *tempo* (fast, slow), *loudness* (loud, soft/quiet), *length of note* (long, short, staccato), and so on.

• Have children choose another familiar song (from memory or the classroom song book) and take turns suggesting how to sing it.

End

• Together with the children, put away the classroom song book and the instruments.

• Use the last song and person/thing chosen by the children to transition to the next activity (e.g., *Let's all sing "Hickory, Dickory, Dock" like a tractor on our way to* [the next activity]).

Ideas for follow-up

• Have the song book in the book area should children want to sing the songs at work/choice time.

• Record children's voices as they sing songs in different ways. Play them back (at recall or next day), and ask children to remember who or what they were trying to represent through their voices. Encourage them to use language related to vocal/musical qualities (e.g., *pitch, tempo,* and *loudness*) to describe and compare their representations.

• Repeat/extend this activity by asking children to sing (or move) like something (e.g., toys, props) in the classroom (e.g., *How would a counting bear sing "The Wheels on the Bus"? How would Sniffy, our guinea pig, move to this music?*).

- At large-group time, encourage children to move to songs and chants as another person or thing. Encourage them to use spatial language to describe and compare their movements (e.g., *I'm raising my arms high on the high parts; Let's turn in a circle whenever we sing the words 'round and 'round*).
- Give the children percussion instruments (e.g., triangles, rhythm sticks, xylophones, drums), and encourage them to imagine different scenarios as they play the instruments (e.g., *What would it sound like if Max and the wild things played these? How about a dog?; Suppose someone was running really fast and playing at the same time — how would that sound?*).

Adaptations for children with special needs

- For children with hearing impairments, use visual cues to help them sing, chant, and keep the beat of songs (e.g., by clapping or patting).

Developmental range: Supporting children at different levels

Earlier →

Children may

- Hum or pat or sway along with the music but not know the words (or know just a few words) of the song.
- Sing the song in their own voice.
- Sing the song the same way each time, without changing their voice to sound like someone or something else.
- Repeat an idea of how to sing the song a different way; imitate someone else's singing.
- Sing the song in one other way (e.g., varying the pitch, tempo, or loudness).
- Comment on their own singing or the singing of someone they know (e.g., *I can sing really fast; Listen how low my voice can go; My daddy likes to sing in the shower*).

Adults can

- Ask *How would it sound if a kitty* (or person or thing suggested by child) *hummed to the song?*
- Comment on change in child's voice (e.g., *You're singing softer this time than you did last time; That's a whole lot faster now!*).
- Imitate how children sing. Ask them if the imitation sounds like them and why (or why not).
- Encourage children to try singing in different voices (e.g., *I wonder how else you can sing; Can I hear some different things you can do with your voice?*).
- Converse with children about their own or other people's singing (e.g., *You sure can sing really fast!; How does your daddy sound when he sings in the shower? What does he like to sing? Do you ever sing with him?*).

Middle →

Children may

- Sing the song in two or more ways.
- Attempt to change their voice to match the person/thing suggested (e.g., lower their voice for a monster and make it higher for a bird; make their voice louder for a dog and softer for a cat; stop and start their voice for a ticking clock).
- Suggest a new variation (e.g., *Sing it like a fish; We could be creepy crawlies*).
- Suggest a new song to sing (e.g., *I wanna sing the one about the mouse and the clock; Sing "Twinkle, Twinkle, Little Star" like the cow that jumped over the moon*).

Adults can

- Comment on/describe the variations in the child's voice. Use a range of vocabulary words related to voice qualities (e.g., *pitch, tempo, loudness, length of note*).
- Ask children, *What should I do with my voice to make it sound like yours* (or the person/thing suggested)*?* Encourage children to use new vocabulary (e.g., pitch, tempo) to describe the qualities of their own and others' voices.
- Imitate inaccurately the sound of a child's voice (e.g., deliberately sing higher or faster) and see if child corrects you; if not, ask *What/how should I sing differently to sound more like you* [or the person/thing suggested]*?*
- Encourage children to listen to and imitate one another's voices. Encourage them to discuss why/how they change their voices to sound like a particular person or thing (e.g., *Let's sing low and quiet like Mira's dog. Now let's try short, loud barks like Ilya's dog. How did you make your voice different?*

Later →

Children may

- Describe how someone or something else would sing the song (e.g., *Sing it low and growly like a dog; A monster would sing really, really loud; How about singing like a train guy and go* toot, toot *at the beginning and the end*).
- Compare how two or more people or things sing (e.g., *A dog has to sing lots louder than a kitty; My mom would sing louder than my dad because she has to yell at us to come for dinner*).

Adults can

- Elaborate on/extend children's suggestions (e.g., *Let's sing like Jamie's monkey, only this time it just woke up from a nap; What if the lion was really hungry — how do you think it would sing "Old MacDonald" then?*).
- Sing a song in a different pitch (or tempo or level of loudness) and encourage children to guess the person/thing singing (e.g., use a high squeaky voice [mouse], quiet voice [kitten], buzzy voice [bee]).
- Extend the child's variation and say, *In what ways do you think my worm* (or person/thing suggested) *sounds different than yours?* Challenge child to sing in a different way than you did (e.g., *I wonder if you can sing like a worm that sounds different than both of us*).

About the Authors

Ann S. Epstein, PhD, is the Senior Director of Curriculum Development at the HighScope Educational Research Foundation in Ypsilanti, Michigan, where she has worked since 1975. She collaborates with a team of early childhood specialists to develop curriculum and staff training materials, develops program and child assessment tools, and evaluates federal, state, and local educational programs. Dr. Epstein has published numerous books and articles for professional and practitioner audiences, including *The Intentional Teacher, Essentials of Active Learning in Preschool,* and *Me, You, Us: Social-Emotional Learning in Preschool,* and is coauthor of *Educating Young Children.* Dr. Epstein is also the principal developer of the *Numbers Plus Preschool Mathematics Curriculum.* She has a PhD in Developmental Psychology from the University of Michigan and also holds a Masters of Fine Arts degree from Eastern Michigan University.

Suzanne Gainsley is a HighScope-certified teacher who has been teaching at the HighScope Demonstration Preschool since 1998. She has also worked with infants, toddlers, preschoolers, and elementary school children in various settings as a teacher, parent, and volunteer. Gainsley is the author of the book *From Message to Meaning: Using a Daily Message Board in the Preschool Classroom,* published by HighScope Press. She is coauthor of two books in the Teacher's Idea Book Series, also from HighScope Press: *"I'm Older Than You. I'm Five!" Math in the Preschool Classroom,* and *50 Large-Group Activities for Active Learners.* Gainsley also writes articles on classroom teaching practices for HighScope's *ReSource* and *Extensions.*

Shannon D. Lockhart, an Early Childhood Specialist and Research Associate with the HighScope Educational Research Foundation since 1988, has served as a national and international researcher, teacher, curriculum developer, trainer, and educational consultant in the United States and abroad. Her areas of expertise include child development (infant-toddler and preschool) and instrument development (observations, program evaluation, and child assessment). A teacher in the HighScope Demonstration Preschool, Lockhart also conducts HighScope infant and toddler and preschool training around the country and abroad. She has written numerous articles for the HighScope publications *Extensions* and *ReSource,* and she authored several chapters in the book *A World of Preschool Experience: Observations in 15 Countries,* published by HighScope Press. She also coproduced the HighScope IEA videotape series, *Sights and Sounds of Preschool Children.* Lockhart holds a master's degree in early childhood education and teaches early childhood courses for Rochester College and Oakland University, both located in Rochester, Michigan.

Beth Marshall is the Interim Director of Early Childhood and Director of the Demonstration Preschool at the HighScope Educational Research Foundation. She has also served as a teacher and mentor in the HighScope Demonstration Preschool and was the coordinator for the HighScope National Diffusion Project through the U.S. Department of Education from 1992–1995. Marshall has written and developed training materials for HighScope on a range of topics, including adult learning, adult-child interactions, and the impact of brain research on early childhood practices. She contributed to the development of the Preschool Child Observation Record (COR) and Program Quality Assessment (PQA) assessment instruments. Marshall also has conducted training projects throughout the United States and internationally and was a trainer and mentor for the inaugural Training of Trainers projects for HighScope Ireland and the Khululeka HighScope Teacher Training Centre in South Africa. She holds a master's degree in early childhood education.

Polly Neill is an Early Childhood Specialist at the HighScope Educational Research Foundation where she has worked for over 20 years. She is the author of *Real Science in Preschool: Here, There, and Everywhere,* published by HighScope Press. Neill was a project codirector in the development and validation of the *Child Observation Record,* and a contributor to *Multicultural Programs* in the Building a HighScope Program Series.

Karen "Kay" Rush is an Early Childhood Specialist at the HighScope Educational Research Foundation where she trains and mentors preschool teachers in the HighScope Curriculum and serves as a substitute teacher at the HighScope Demonstration Preschool. Rush is the author of *Head Start Preschool Programs* in the Building a

HighScope Program Series, published by HighScope Press; she also writes articles for HighScope's publications, *ReSource* and *Extensions.*

Before joining HighScope, Rush worked her way up through the ranks of Head Start, beginning, in 1981, as an assistant teacher and progressing to teacher, center administrator, assistant education coordinator, and education coordinator. She holds a bachelor's degree in sign language studies and a master's degree in early childhood education. A licensed minister, Rush is the founder and director of Lift Up Your Hands Ministries, where she directs a community sign-mime choir that ministers to hearing and Deaf audiences using American Sign Language and pantomime with Gospel, Christian, and inspirational music.

Resources From High/Scope

The High/Scope Preschool Curriculum

From essential basics to research-validated details, our curriculum provides all the know-how you need for running a high-quality program. You've been asking for a user-friendly introduction to High/Scope — now it's here! Every professor, center director, and classroom should still have a copy of our in-depth curriculum manual, *Educating Young Children,* but every college student, classroom teacher, and administrator will want a copy of *Essentials of Active Learning in Preschool* as a practical daily guide!

We have also created a program called High/Scope Step by Step to help you get started. These steps include recommendations for products and training at each step you choose to take. High/Scope Step by Step offers you an affordable and achievable plan for curriculum implementation. For more information, see the High/Scope Web site at *www.highscope.org.*

Essentials of Active Learning in Preschool: Getting to Know the High/Scope Curriculum

This guide presents a comprehensive introduction to the High/Scope Preschool Curriculum, covering theory and research, teaching practices, curriculum content, assessment, and training. It offers an appealing format that includes examples, checklists, teacher anecdotes, and hands-on exercises. The book also serves as a practical guide to help you implement High/Scope's active learning approach.

Whether you are planning to adopt the High/Scope Curriculum or are just looking for information on what it takes to have a successful active learning environment, this book is a must-have for all early childhood administrators and educators as well as students preparing to enter the field.

BK-P1335

A. S. Epstein. Soft cover, photos, 243 pages. 978-1-57379-300-1

Educating Young Children: Active Learning Practices for Preschool and Child Care Programs (3rd Ed.)

Completely revised and updated, this manual is still the most complete guide to the High/Scope Preschool Curriculum and a classic in the field that no early childhood professional should be without. Written for teachers, administrators, teacher-trainers, college students, and professors, the manual describes indispensable strategies for effective early childhood education. The third edition reflects High/Scope's new curriculum content framework based on 58 key developmental indicators (KDIs) organized in categories that closely parallel state and professional early childhood standards.

Topics include planning the physical setting; establishing a consistent daily routine that includes plan-do-review and small- and large-group times; using adult scaffolding and support strategies to help children acquire essential skills and concepts; establishing family partnerships; and team planning. The book explores in-depth the new KDIs that make up the High/Scope curriculum content areas for preschoolers: approaches to learning; language, literacy, and communication; social and emotional development; physical development, health, and well-being; mathematics; science and technology; social studies; and the arts. This new edition reflects both the latest research on early learning and time-tested educational practices based on more than 40 years of rigorous studies coupled with classroom innovation. Complete with photos, checklists, sample classroom plans, and real-life scenarios. Includes the latest findings of High/Scope's landmark Perry Preschool Study.

BK-P1356

M. Hohmann, D. P. Weikart, & A. S. Epstein. Soft cover, photos, 560 pages. 978-1-57379-354-4

Order online: *www.highscope.org*

High/Scope Offers Ideas Galore for Teachers and Child Care Providers!

High/Scope Step by Step: Lesson Plans for the First 30 Days

This appealing guide puts 30 days of ready-to-use High/Scope lesson plans right at your fingertips! For teachers new to High/Scope, this book will help you get started by providing 6 weeks of user-friendly plans. Teachers experienced with High/Scope will find the book a ready source of new ideas. Each lesson plan includes activities for greeting time, plan-do-review, and small- and large-group times. Most of the plans offer additional ideas for outside time, meal conversations, and/or parent involvement. The book also includes a music CD, tips, adult-child interaction strategies, and reproducible lesson planning sheets to help teachers learn to create an active learning environment step by step!

BK-P1346
B. Marshall with S. Lockhart & M. Fewson. Soft cover, 184 pages. 978-1-57379-320-9

Explore and Learn Quick Cards: 50 Activities for Large Groups

This set is the second in the *Explore and Learn Quick Cards* series. Each durable, easy-to-use card contains a large-group activity plan that describes the originating idea; the materials needed; the curriculum content areas; and the process for conducting the activity, including an opener, the main part of the activity, the transition to the next activity, variations, follow-up suggestions, and accommodations for children with special needs. Colorful dividers organize the activities into five sections:

• Easy-to-join activities for starting large-group times
• Songs, fingerplays, and chants
• Storytelling and story reenactments
• Movement activities
• Cooperative games and projects

Additional cards describe numerous teaching strategies for planning and conducting large-group activities. The cards are three-hole drilled to fit in a notebook and may also be stored in hanging files in a file cabinet or in the High/Scope Teacher Resources box. The cards include the activities found in the *50 Large-Group Activities for Active Learners* book.

BK-P1353
C. Boisvert & S. Gainsley. Photos, 60 cards, 7 dividers. 978-1-57379-349-0

Explore and Learn Quick Cards: 80 Activities for Small Groups

Each of these handy, durable, and easy-to-use cards contains practical suggestions and detailed descriptions to help teachers create active learning small groups. The set of cards includes a vibrant High/Scope Teacher Resources label as well as dividers that organize the activities. The cards are conveniently sized to fit in hanging files in the High/Scope Teacher Resources Box or a file cabinet, and they are three-hole drilled for those who prefer to store them in a binder. The *Explore and Learn Quick Cards* include many of the activities found in the *100 Small-Group Experiences* book and more.

BK-P1337
M. Graves. Photos, 80 activity cards, 6 dividers. 978-1-57379-311-7

Order online: *www.highscope.org*

The Teacher's Idea Book Series

Real Science in Preschool: Here, There, and Everywhere

Wondering how to "do science" with preschoolers? This latest volume in the Teacher's Idea Book series shows you how authentic, hands-on science learning takes place every day throughout the classroom as well as outdoors. You'll learn to recognize and support the six behaviors that are part of the preschool scientific method (observing, classifying, experimenting, predicting, drawing conclusions, and communicating ideas) that you'll see in all types of children's play — behaviors that lay the groundwork for children's later science learning in school. Introductory chapters provide an overview of early science learning and supportive adult-child interactions, while later chapters take you on a tour of classroom interest areas to find the science learning going on and consider strategies and materials that encourage children's ideas. Also includes information on creating science-related group-time activities based on children's interests and templates for developing your own group-time activities.

BK-P1366 P. Neill. Soft cover, photos, approx. 170 pages. 978-1-57379-364-3

"I Know What's Next!" Preschool Transitions Without Tears or Turmoil

This book provides guidelines that help teachers understand transitions from the child's point of view, along with a host of strategies, songs, games, and other experiences that are useful for particular transitions. Included are ideas for drop-off and pick-up times; the times before and after each part of the daily routine, including wait times; cleanup time; room-to-room transitions; and the transition to kindergarten. Also offered are parent handouts, real-life transition scenarios, photos, and illustrations with adult-child dialogues depicting contrasting approaches to transitions.

BK-P1336 B. Evans. Soft cover, photos and illustrations, 116 pages. 978-1-57379-297-4

50 Large-Group Activities for Active Learners

This book presents 50 engaging large-group activities that stimulate children's creativity, help them learn skills and concepts, and introduce them to a wide range of new and thought-provoking experiences. Designed for early childhood professionals seeking to accommodate children's interests and initiatives, this book contains valuable ideas for action songs, group storytelling, movement activities, and cooperative games and projects.

BK-P1316 C. Boisvert & S. Gainsley. Soft cover, photos, 139 pages. 978-1-57379-282-0

Save by purchasing as a set with our Large-Group Times for Active Learners Video or DVD! Visit *www.highscope.org* for details.

"I'm Older Than You. I'm Five!" Math in the Preschool Classroom

Young children need math concepts presented intentionally and systematically, yet in a way that also respects their concrete thinking and their need to learn by exploring hands-on materials. This book presents 50 early math activities that meet these needs for preschoolers. Aligned with the early childhood standards of the National Council of Teachers of Mathematics (NCTM), these activities will help children gain competence in early math key experiences.

BK-P1248 A. Epstein & S. Gainsley. Soft cover, 179 pages. 978-1-57379-221-9

Making the Most of Plan-Do-Review

This book includes support strategies for the plan-do-review process including practical tips and suggestions, tried-and-true games and experiences for children, answers to frequently asked questions, real-life examples, sample notes to parents, a parent workshop plan, and planning and recall sheets to use with children.

BK-P1152 N. Vogel. Soft cover, photos, 250 pages. 1-57379-086-9

The Teacher's Idea Book Series

The Essential Parent Workshop Resource

Presenters will find it easy to follow the format of these 30 original workshops, which include intended goals, a list of necessary materials, an introduction and interactive opening activity, central ideas for discussion, scenarios for reflection and application of ideas, and follow-up plans that encourage parents to apply the information at home.

BK-P1137 M. Graves. Soft cover, photos, 180 pages. 978-1-57379-018-5

100 Small-Group Experiences

Packed with suggestions teachers can use to provide 100 exciting, active learning small groups. Activities are presented in four sections: children's interests, new materials, the important content areas in child development, and community experiences.

BK-P1115 M. Graves. Soft cover, photos, 220 pages. 1-57379-029-X

Planning Around Children's Interests

An essential handbook for dedicated professionals, this book is filled with practical teaching strategies and actual classroom examples of teacher-child interactions. Fun for all, the ideas draw on children's interests as a rich resource for curriculum planning.

BK-P1106 M. Graves. Soft cover, photos, 171 pages. 1-57379-019-2

Conflict Resolution

You Can't Come to My Birthday Party! Conflict Resolution With Young Children

This book presents a six-step mediation process adults can use to help young children resolve disputes. More than 50 scenarios of conflict resolution in action are included.

BK-P1171 B. Evans. Soft cover, photos, 432 pages. 978-1-57379-159-5

Supporting Children in Resolving Conflicts

This important video will demonstrate the six problem-solving steps with real scenes of successful conflict resolution from a New York City Head Start Center and from the High/Scope Demonstration Preschool.

Video: BK-P1130 Color, 30 minutes, viewer guide included. 1-57379-042-7
DVD: BK-P1300 1-57379-247-0

Steps in Resolving Conflicts Wall-Size Poster

Hang this poster in your classroom to help you remember the six steps to resolving conflicts as you work with children.

BK-P1134 Two-color glossy, 22" x 34". 1-57379-075-3

Steps in Resolving Conflicts Small-Size Poster, English-Spanish

Hang these laminated small-size posters in your classroom and/or your parent area to help adults remember the six steps to resolving conflicts as they interact with children. Spanish version on the other side.

BK-P1365 Set of 2 posters, two-color, glossy, 8½" x 11". 978-1-57379-408-4

Order online: *www.highscope.org*